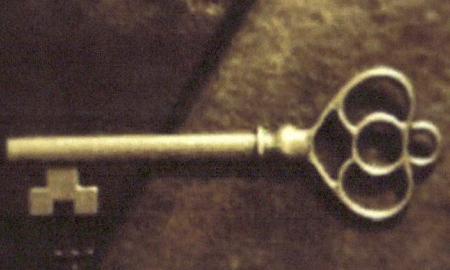

God's 7 Keys for Creative People

WRITTEN AND ILLUSTRATED BY TONY SNIPES

2

ArtLessonsFromGod.com Presents:

God's 7 Keys
for
Creative People

Written & Illustrated By
Tony Snipes

Published By
Kreative Kingdom, Inc.
Inman, South Carolina

This book is dedicated to the memory of the "real"
Edward B. Garrett, my grandfather.

I remember him as a man of few words,
and a very hard worker that didn't ask for much in return.
I can only wonder what his inner most dreams were.
No matter how the world measures "success",
his quiet life was still significant.

Let this book serve as a method
of the world hearing his name.

CONTENTS

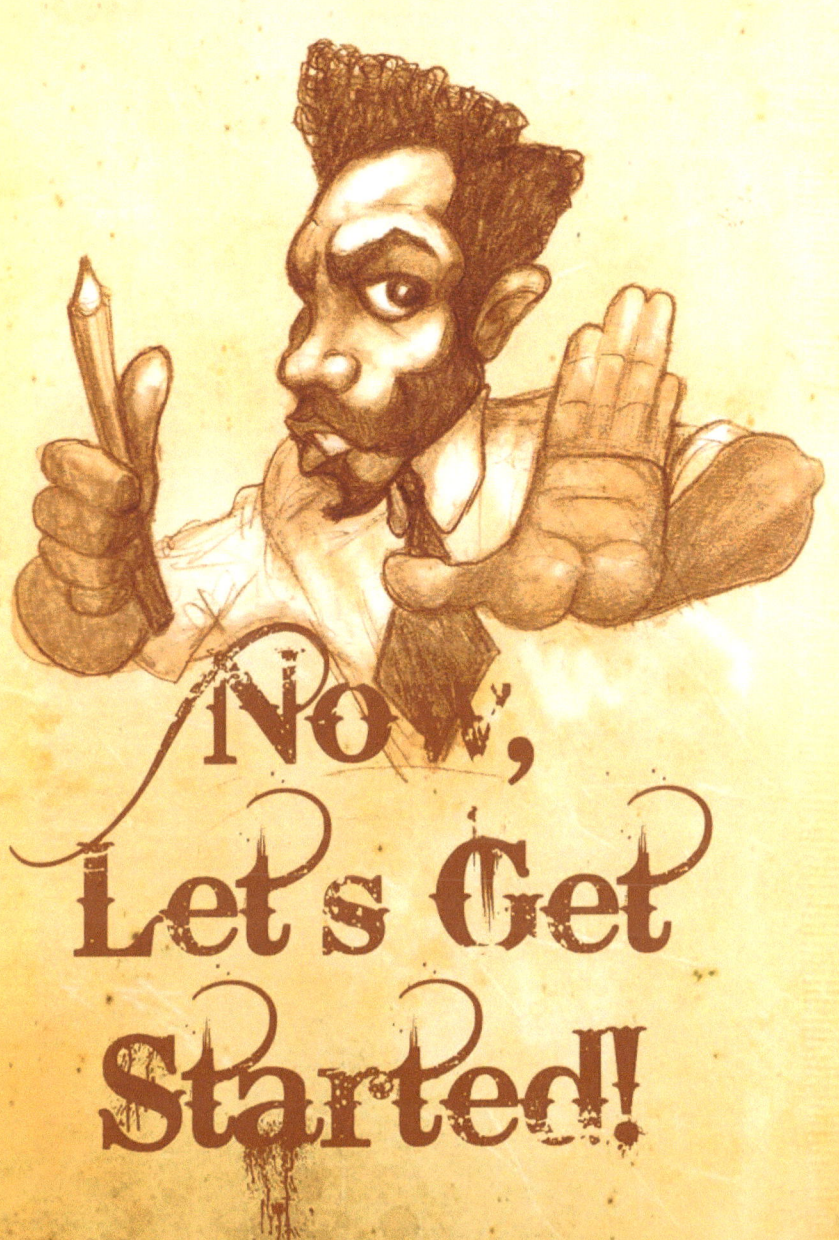

Now, Let's Get Started!!

SO, WHO IS EDWARD B. GARRETT?

I realized that authoring a book FOR creative people ABOUT their creativity had to be approached in (of all things) a creative manner.

That is why I chose to design this book as the account of early twentieth century artist, designer and inventor Edward B. Garrett.

In his pursuit for the answers to the three questions we all have asked:

Who am I?
Why am I here?
What should I be doing?

...Edward discovered 7 biblically based principles related to his faith and his creative talent that address those 3 questions.

Edward refers to those 7 principles as "keys" because these principles, like keys:

Symbolize authority (a person with keys usually is in charge of what they open).

Grant access to things not everyone has access to.

Lock out and keep secure.

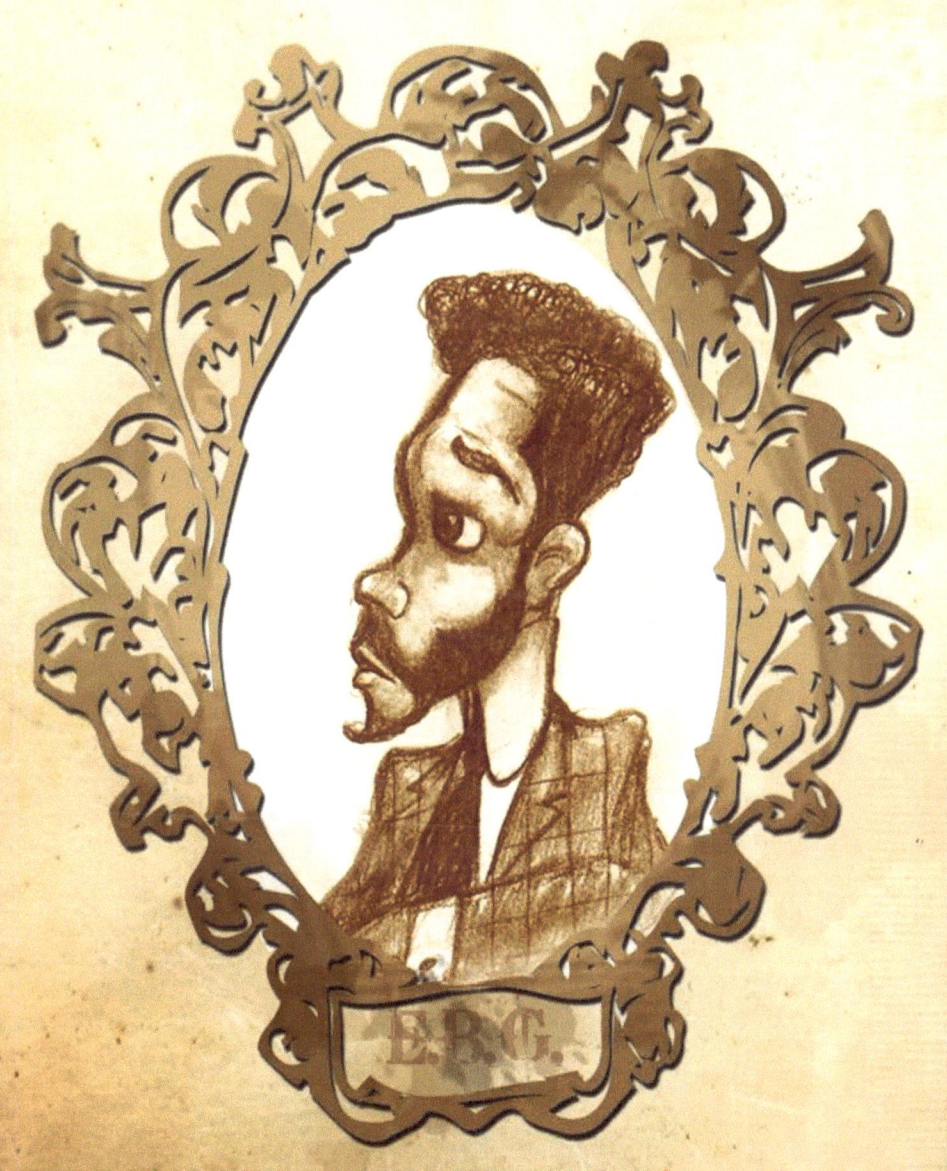

E.R.G.

What People are Saying About this Book

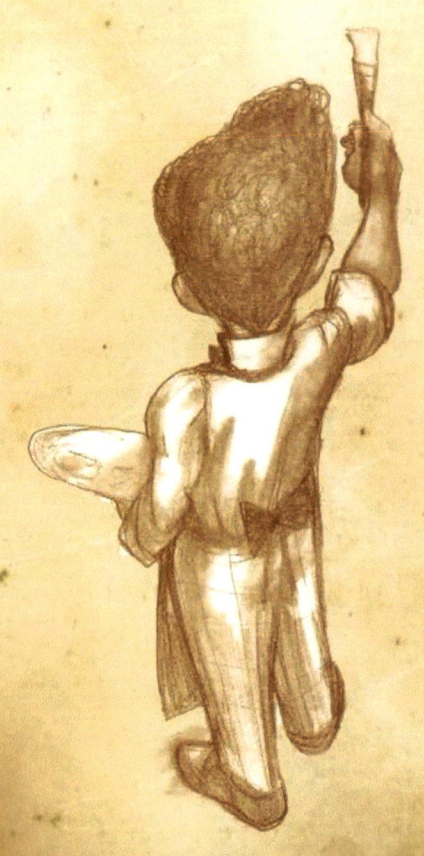

"Tony Snipes has tapped into the mind of the Creator to connect to those He created. This book shares the insight on the power and potential that can be released in the earth when these two elements reunite and the tragedy that could continue if they don't."

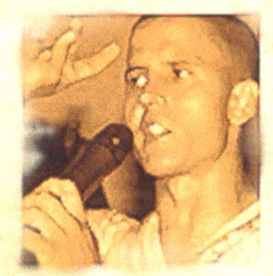

**Mike Darnell Lead Pastor,
Excel Church
www.ExcelChurchAtlanta.com**

"Tony Snipes, a man of many gifts, has just written a blueprint for the creative mind. 'God's 7 Keys for Creative People' will open your eyes. Tony Snipes is handing you the keys."

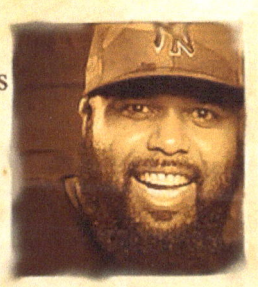

**Pastor Brian M. Ellis
Connections Pastor, RWOC**

"In his book, 'God's 7 Keys for Creative People', Tony Snipes has brought such clarity to the reader. This book will enlighten the reader who has never understood the purpose for their gift, talent, and creativity."

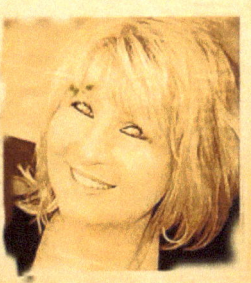

**Karyl Gaehring
Founder, God Invasion**

"As a multi-media artist 'God's 7 Keys for Creative People' has sparked a creative flame and awakened my creative spirit when I thought my creativity had come to a standstill."

Jeremy Goldsmith, Author, Speaker & Multi-media Artist
wwwPushBrokers.com

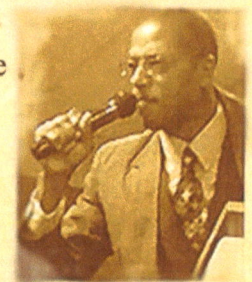

"'God's 7 Keys for Creative People' does an excellent job of highlighting biblical principles as they are directly related to the arts. It not only recognizes God as the original creator, but also shares the artistic inheritance we are given as children of God."

Nachae' Jones,
Entrepreneur/Prophetic Artist
www.rhemawordphotos.com

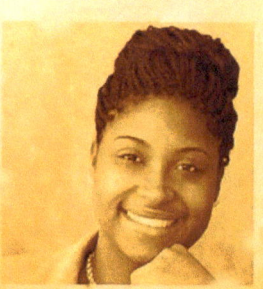

"This quick yet informative read offers artists with the fundamental truths about what it means to be creating with a purpose. Being creative is a gift that one must put to use. Tony Snipes gives us a glimpse at where that gift comes from and what we should be doing with it in this life."

Biljana Kroll, Artist, Instructor
www.biljanakroll.com

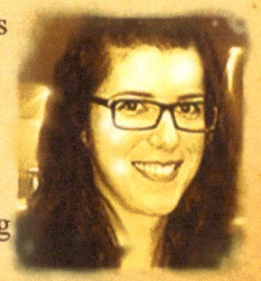

"In this short book, insightful artist Tony Snipes reminds us of 7 powerful keys to successfully creating with God."

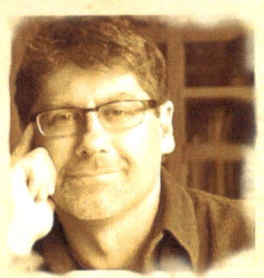

**J. Scott McElroy, Author,
'Creative Church Handbook' and 'Finding Divine Inspiration'
www.jscottmcelroy.com**

"Tony your manuscript is on point and on time. You gave me a WOW moment, thank you for such a refreshing look at the Arts."

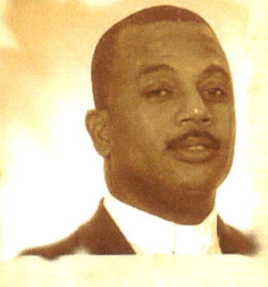

**William Norman, Jr.
Pastor of Proctor Hill Baptist Church
Bluffton, SC**

" 'God's 7 Keys for Creative People' allows you to dive deep and get to the root of your artistic calling. It takes you by the hand and guides you through the journey of discovering your purpose and how to walk it out."

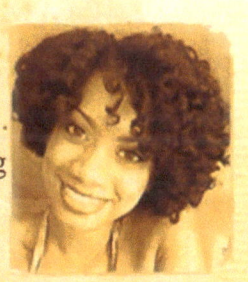

**Stacey Smith,
Smit'N Photography**

"In his book 'God's 7 Keys for Creative People', Tony addresses the three questions creative people have been asking almost from Eden. Who am I? Why I am here? and What Should I be doing?"

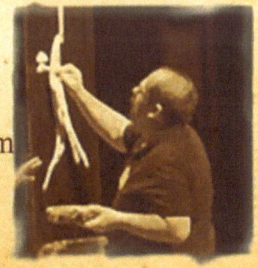

**Dave Weiss,
www.amokarts.com**

13

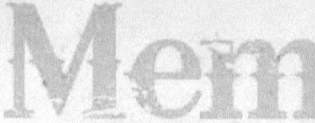

PULLING BACK THE CURTAIN

If I were to pull back the curtain and allow you a glimpse of what the invisible spirit realm looked like, it would look less like a world of clouds, mist and vaporous specters floating as they followed human beings.

It is my belief that the invisible spirit realm we often wonder about in mystery is actually made up of things more familiar to us than we could ever know.

Pulling back the curtain would show us that the spirit realm is vastly made up of:

THOUGHTS
IDEAS
MEMORIES
and FEELINGS

Invisible...but not so mysterious. On the contrary, very familiar things that are woven within our day-to-day lives.

What does a thought look like?
Is an idea real even though you can't see it?
I see a memory right now, but I can not touch it.
Feelings live silently within you, but do they ever make you speak?

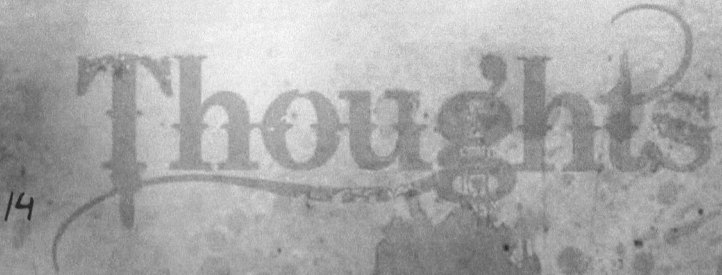

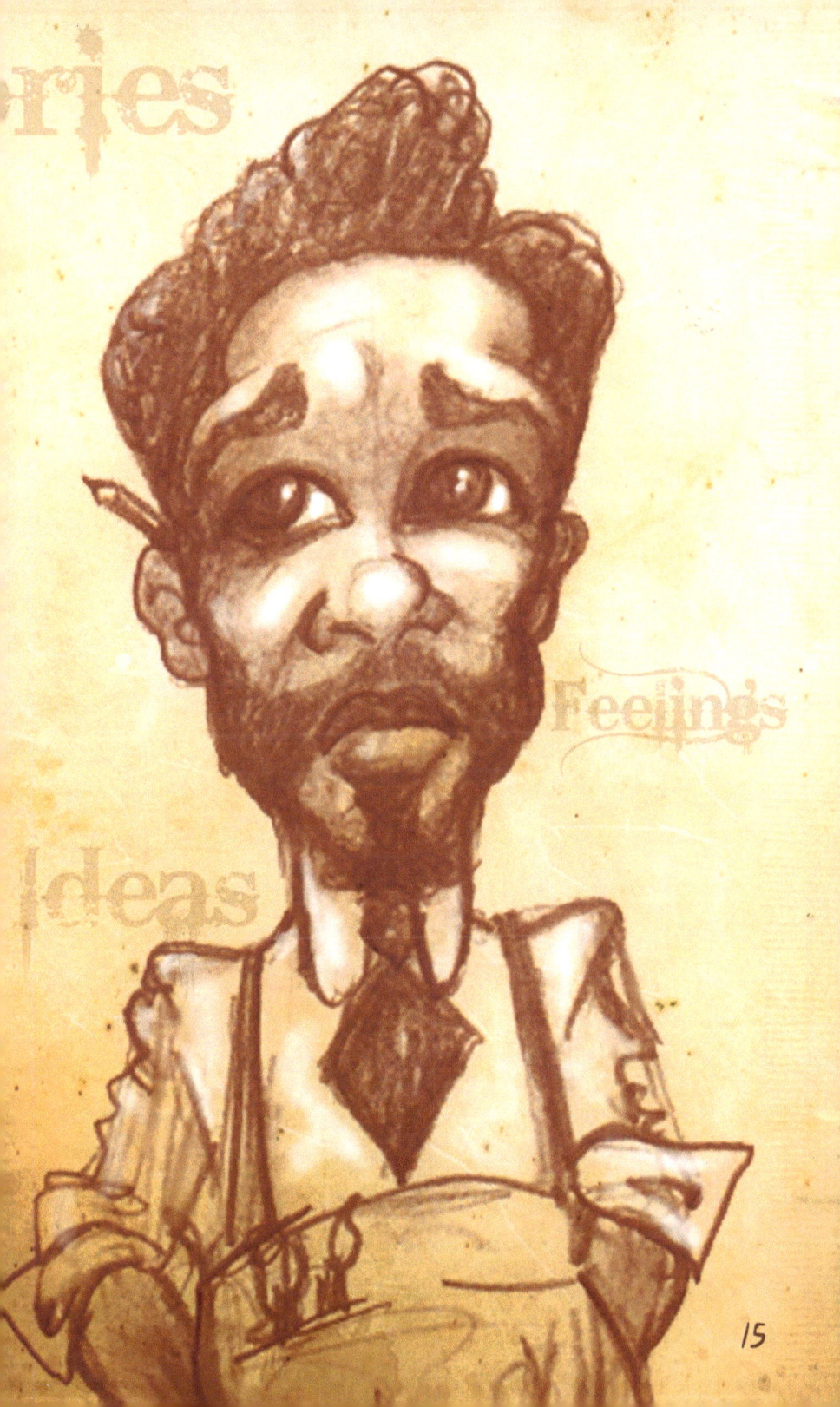

15

All of these invisible (spirit realm) things have immediate impact on the visible (natural realm) world.

Nothing moves in the visible world without the influence of the invisible.

AND THIS is why creative people are so important to the kingdom of God...and to the kingdom darkness.

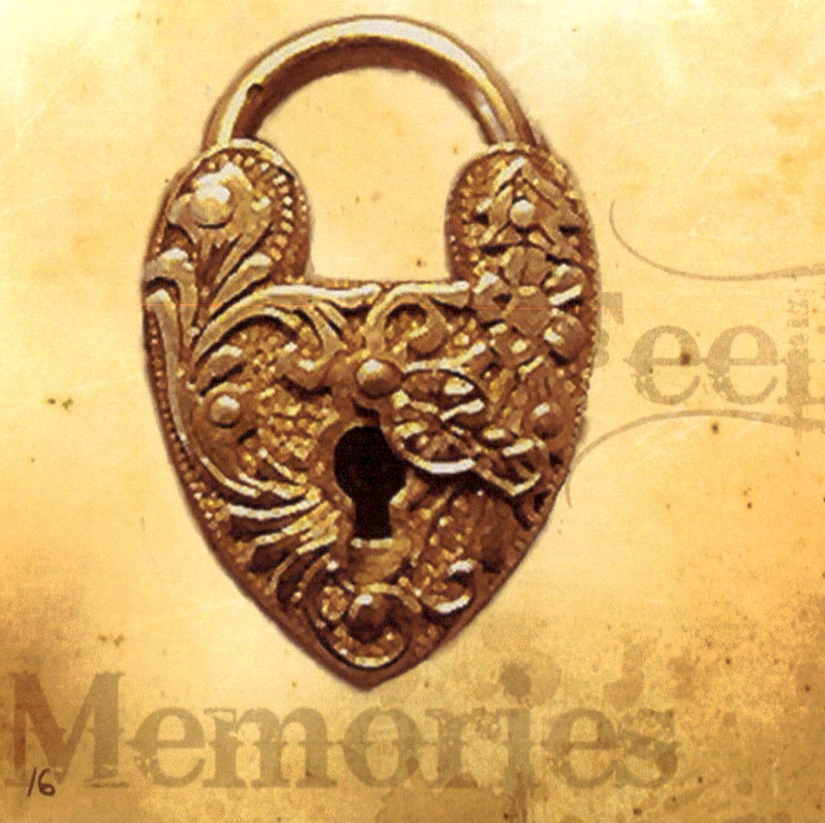

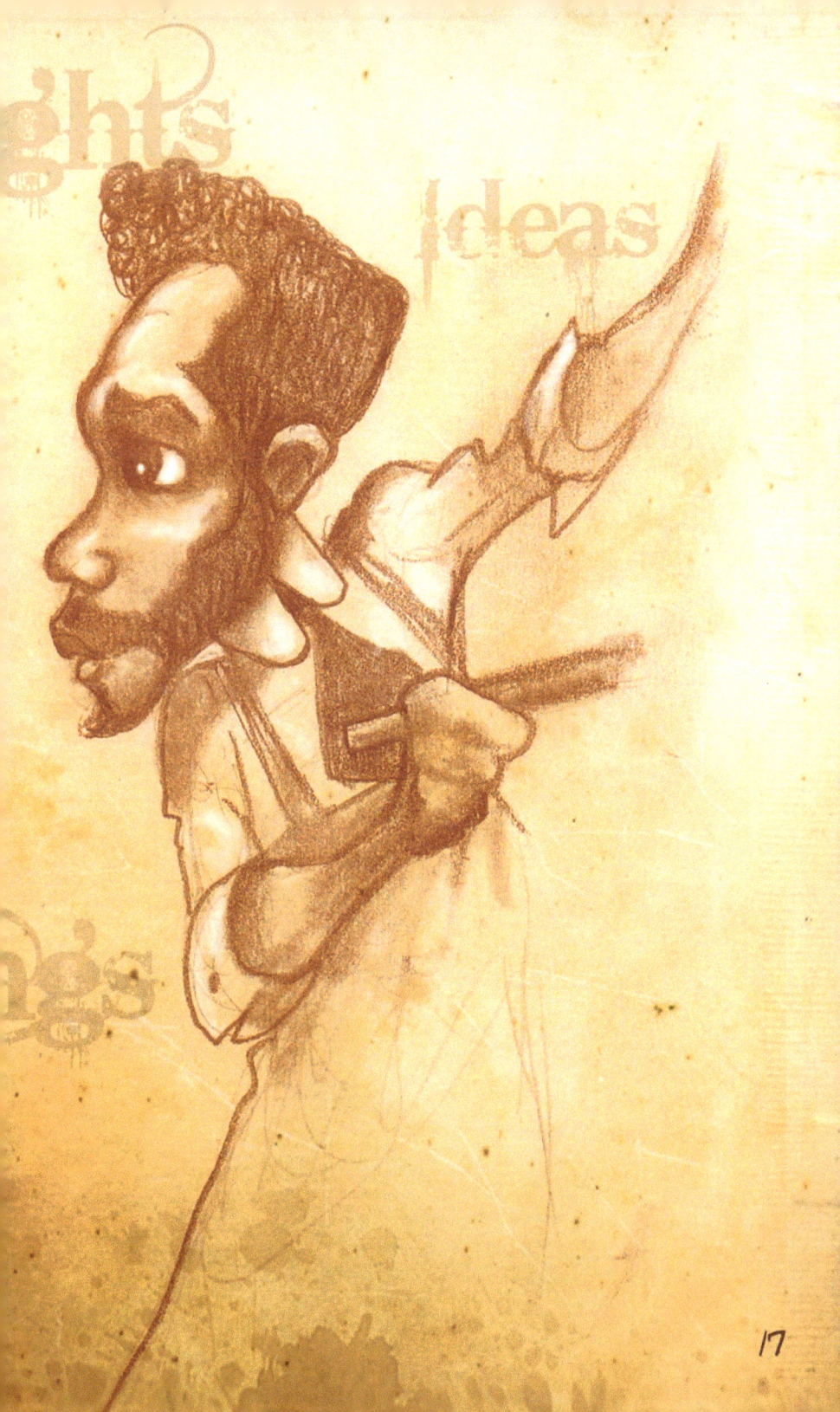

THERE'S A WAR GOING ON...

I believe your adversary will BATTLE to either GAIN ACCESS to your creativity and its influence...or to DISTRACT you from using it at all. Your talent is POWERFUL...like a high powered reactor

When used for good, it can light up an entire city! ...but when misused, that reactor can destroy that same city.

And why would our talent be so powerful? Because the ability to create is a gift directly from God; and anything from God has power.

Why do you think the enemy tries to latch on to musicians, writers, designers, etc? Because creatives are the thought influencers. And he who controls the creatives of a society controls the mind of that society.

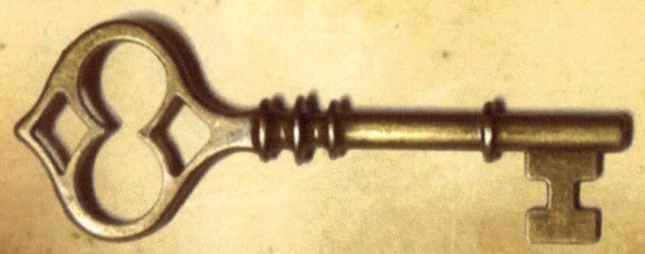

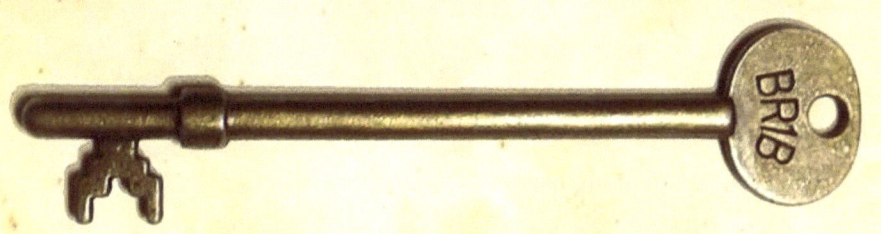

HERE'S HOW IT WORKS:

1. Art, music, design, etc. evokes emotions, memories, concepts and THOUGHTS.

2. THOUGHTS lead to ACTIONS

3. ACTIONS repeated, lead to HABITS (some good, some bad)

4. HABITS repeated lead to LIFESTYLE

And thus is the reason why the enemy wants to either own or stop your creativity…so that he can influence you to influence others for his purpose, or keep you from impacting the lives of others with your creative talent for the good.

Yes, I believe we are approaching the biggest battle in the culture war more than ever before. And it is my hope that these seven principles…these seven KEYS will position you to walk in victory!

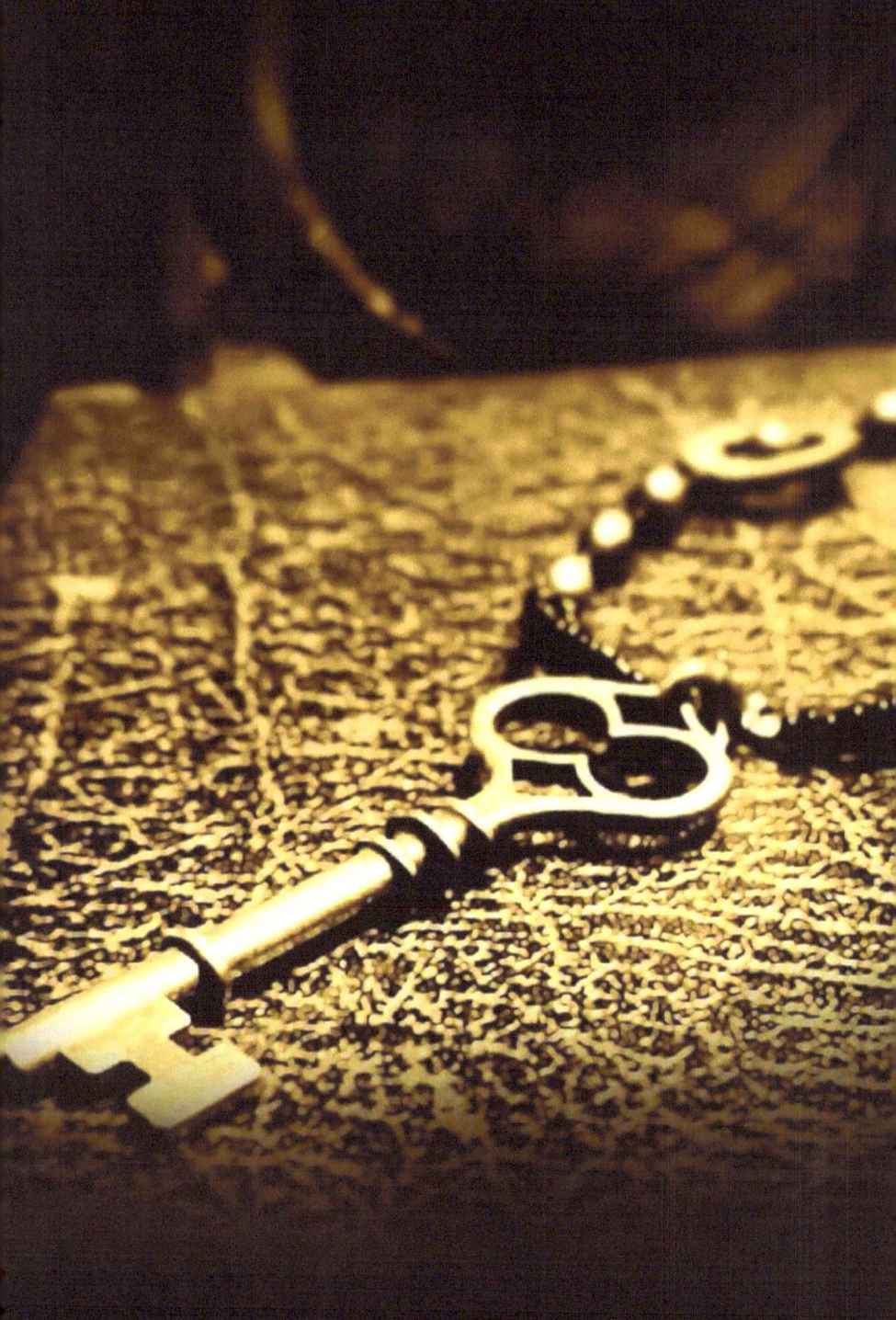

Creative Key Number 1

God is a creative God.

The first thing that we learn about God's personality is that He is creative.

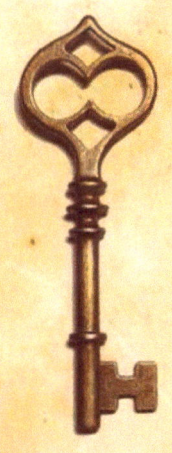

"God is a creative God.
The first thing that we learn about the personality of God is that He is creative."

-Edward B. Garrett

"In the beginning God created the heavens and the earth. Now the earth was formless and empty, darkness was over the surface of the deep, and the Spirit of God was hovering over the waters..... (continues)"
Genesis 1:1-31

The first thing that God reveals to us about His personality is that He is a very creative God. The first 5 words in the Bible are "In The Beginning God Created-".

This shows the creative person how there are many similarities between himself and the One that gave him his talent in the first place.

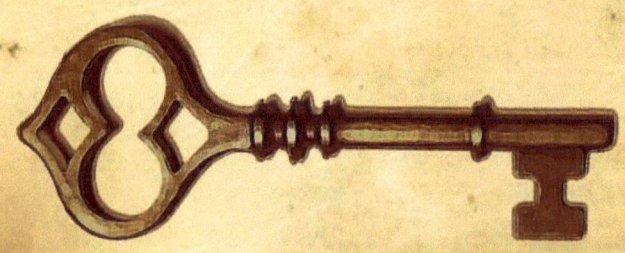

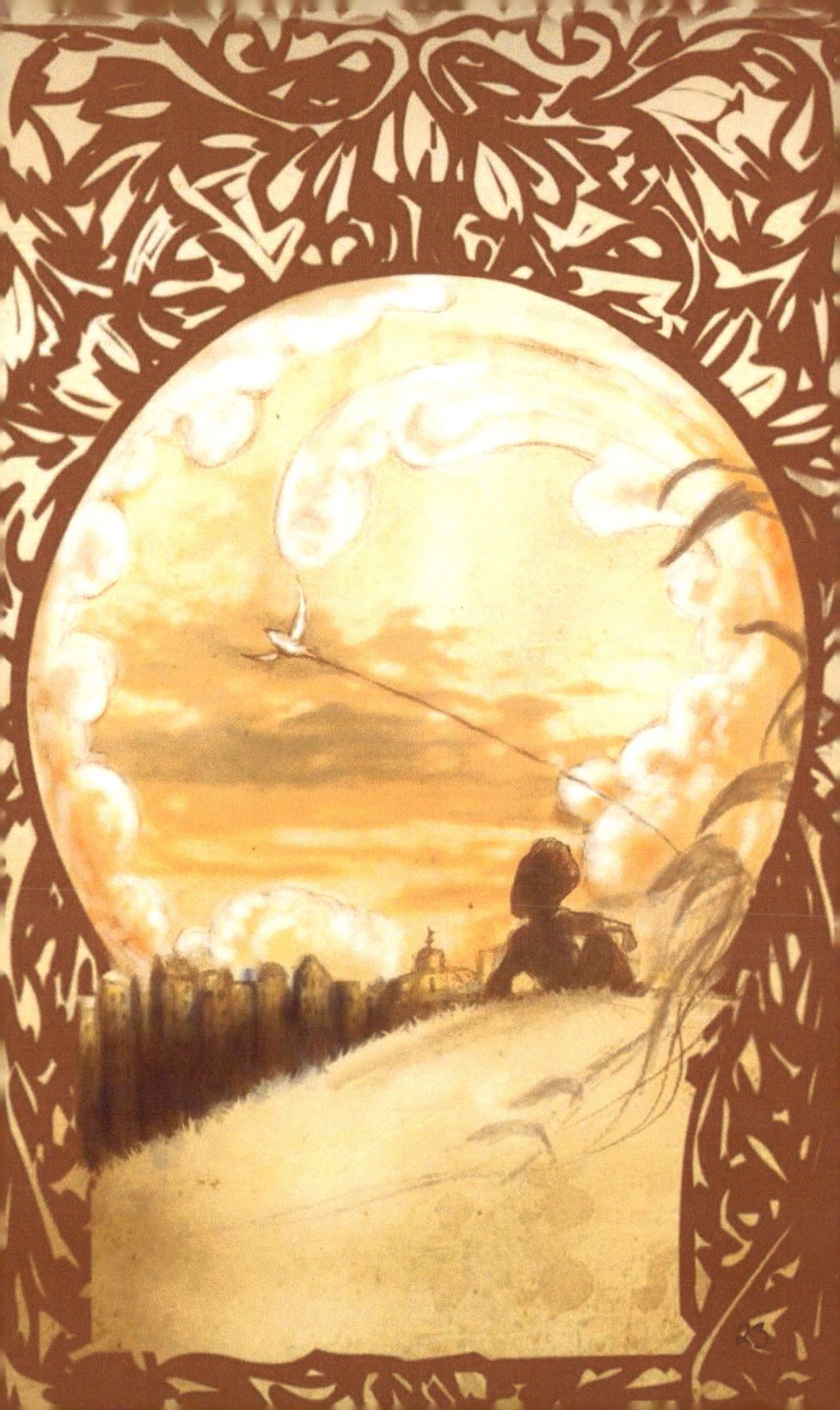

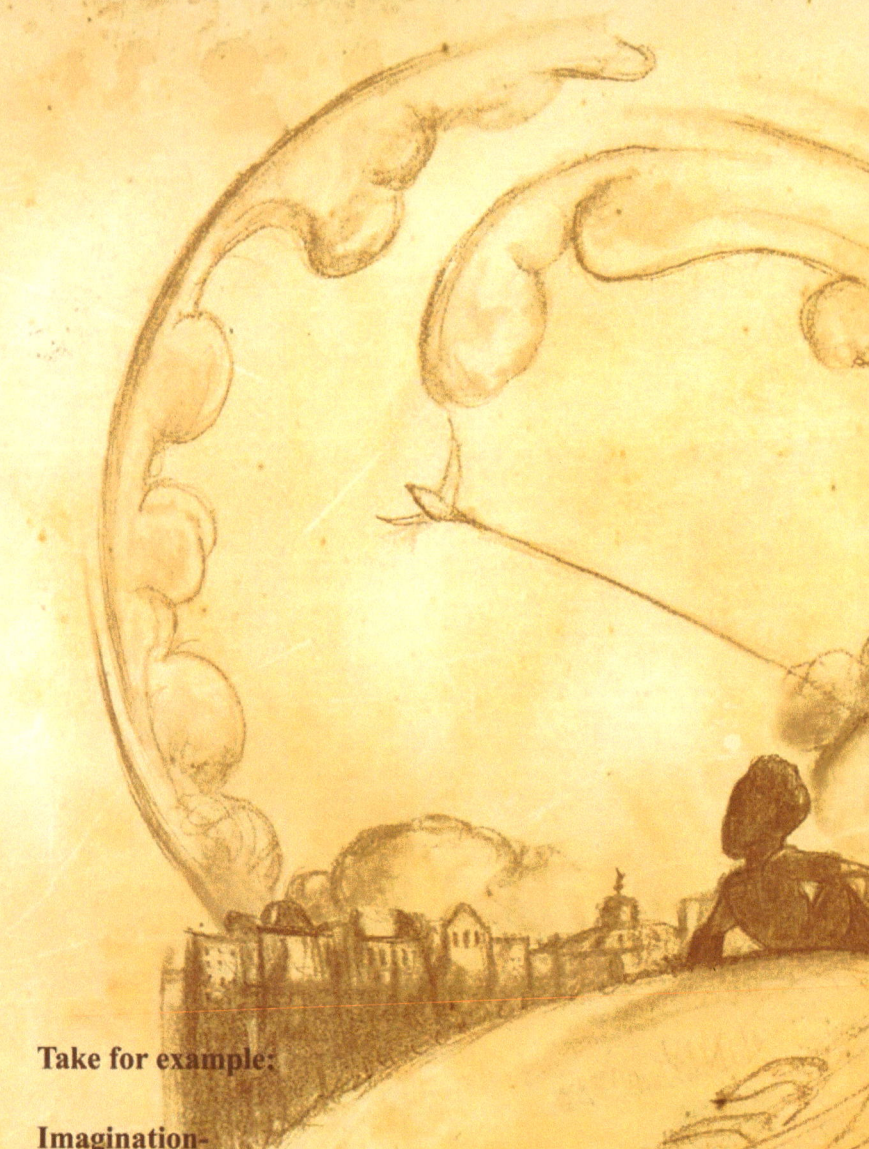

Take for example:

Imagination-
 If you are like most creatives, you usually find yourself imagining the thing you will create first before you create it. The ability to visualize and see the unseen before you create it is a special and unique ability. You may find yourself the only person who can "see" the design, the image or whatever that invisible thing is. That's your imagination.

24

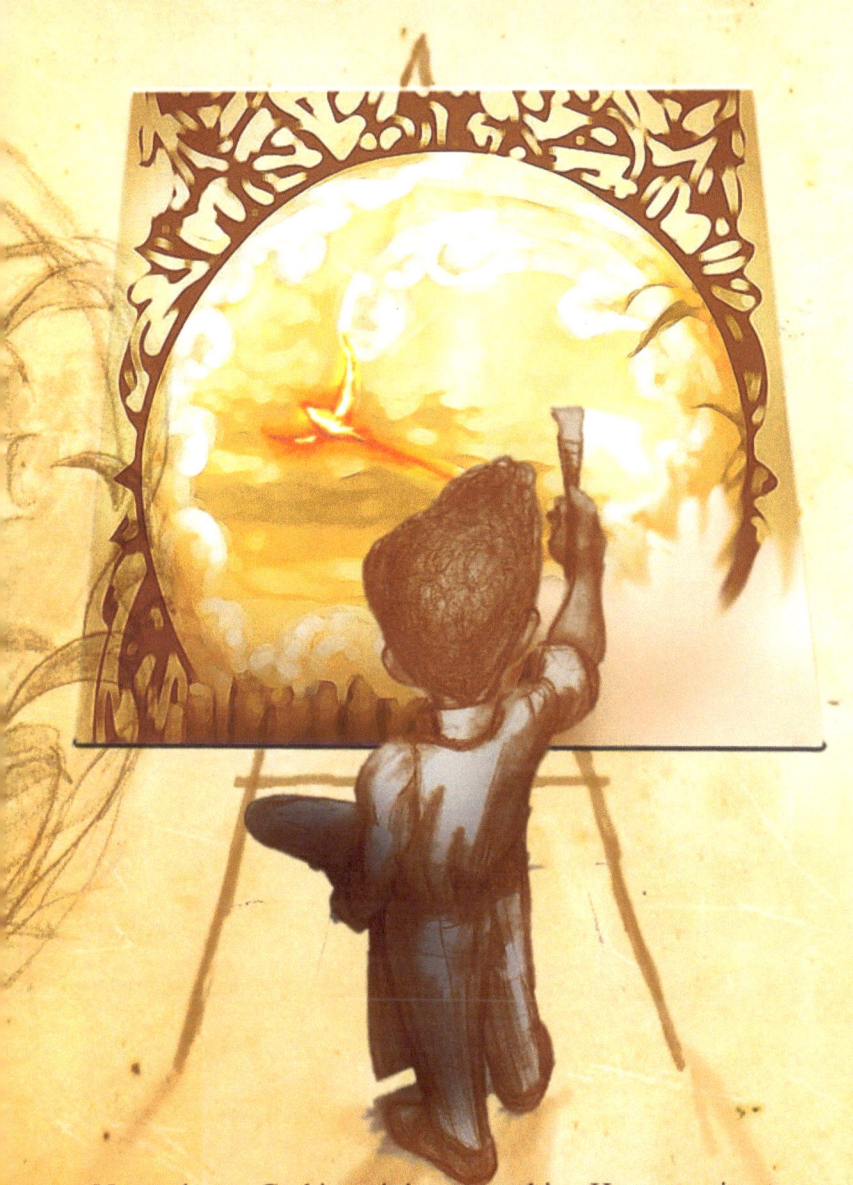

Now, picture God imagining everything He was going to create before He actually created it, how He wants it to look, the colors…sound familiar? In the first chapter of Genesis, God imagines the creation, it comes into being, and He checks it out and gives His stamp of approval because it's just the way He imagined it in the first place: "Let there be light…and there was light…and God saw that the light was good."

So, we see the creative side of God before seeing anything else about Him. A creative God with an imagination. A designer who measures His work based on how He first imagined it. This shows the creative that these same shared traits originated from your creator.

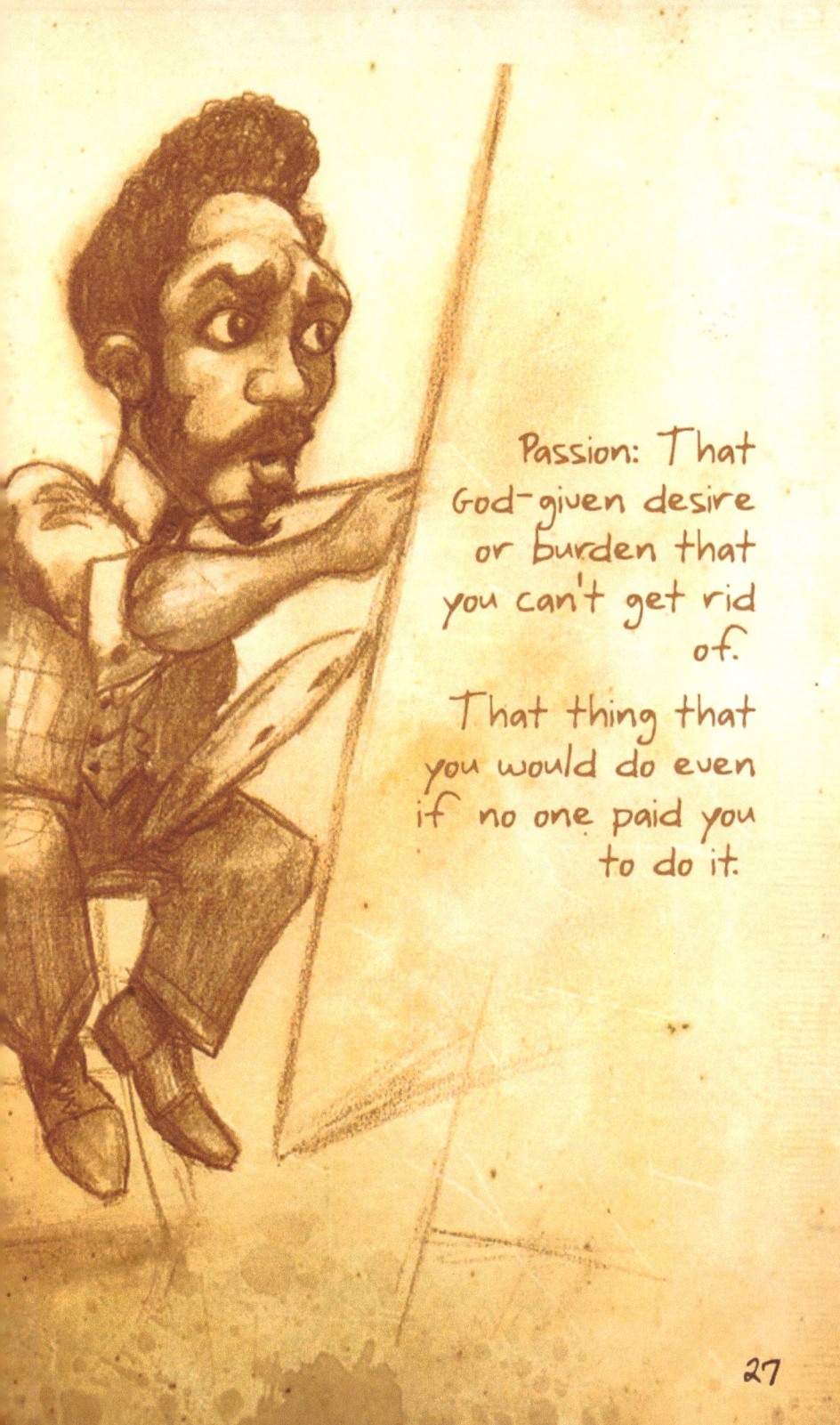

Passion: That God-given desire or burden that you can't get rid of.

That thing that you would do even if no one paid you to do it.

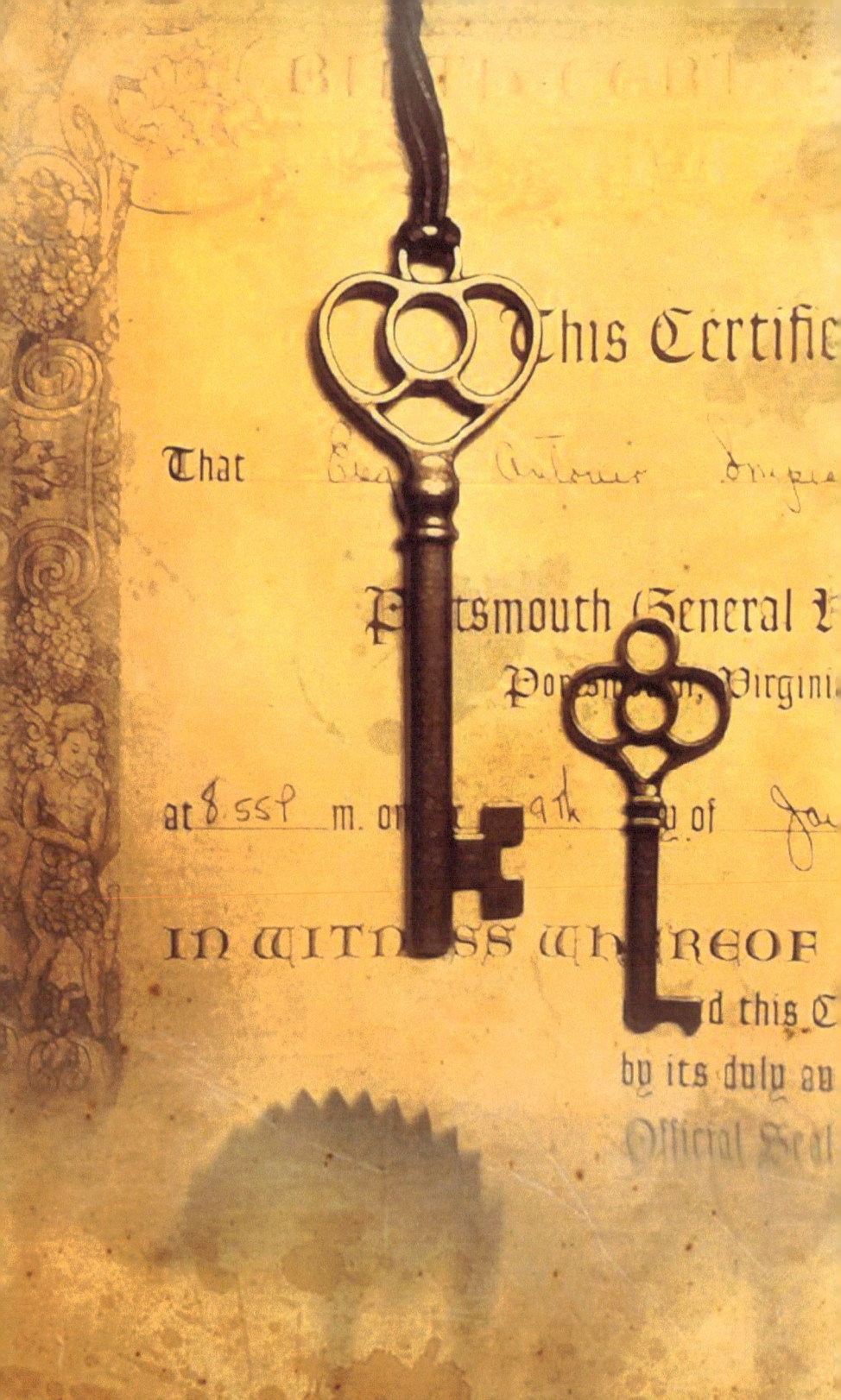

Creative Key Number 2

God created you in His image.
He designed you to be creative
just like He is.

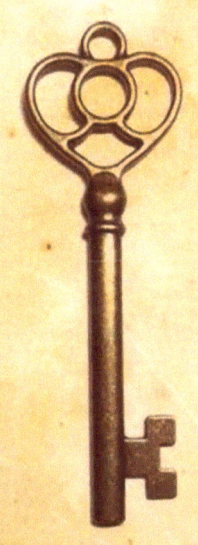

God created you in His image. He designed you to be creative just like He is."

-Edward B. Garrett

"Then God said, 'Let us make man in our image, in our likeness, and let them rule over the fish of the sea and the birds of the air, over the livestock, over all the earth, and over all the creatures that move along the ground.' So God created man in his own image,
in the image of God he created him; male and female he created them."

Genesis 1:26-27

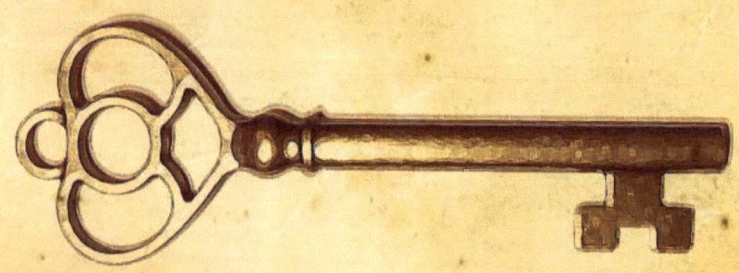

Edward
B.
Garrett
Artisan
1900

#Gods7keys   31

God made you in 2 ways:

1. In His image
2. And in His likeness

What's the difference?

Image- means you are God's Representative on Earth.
This is like a Manager. A manager runs the business for The
Boss! He has been given power and authority by the Boss
to run things just like the Boss would run things.

Likeness- means you have similar ways or a nature like
God's nature (such as being creative)! Notice out of every
creature that God created, we are the only one that can
imagine, design and create any form of artistic
expression…just like Him.

An example of Likeness can be found with a parent and
their child. Many children grow to behave and even look
like their parents. That is because part of the parent (genes,
etc.) is actually inside the child! Many artists have parents
or children that are artistic like they are.

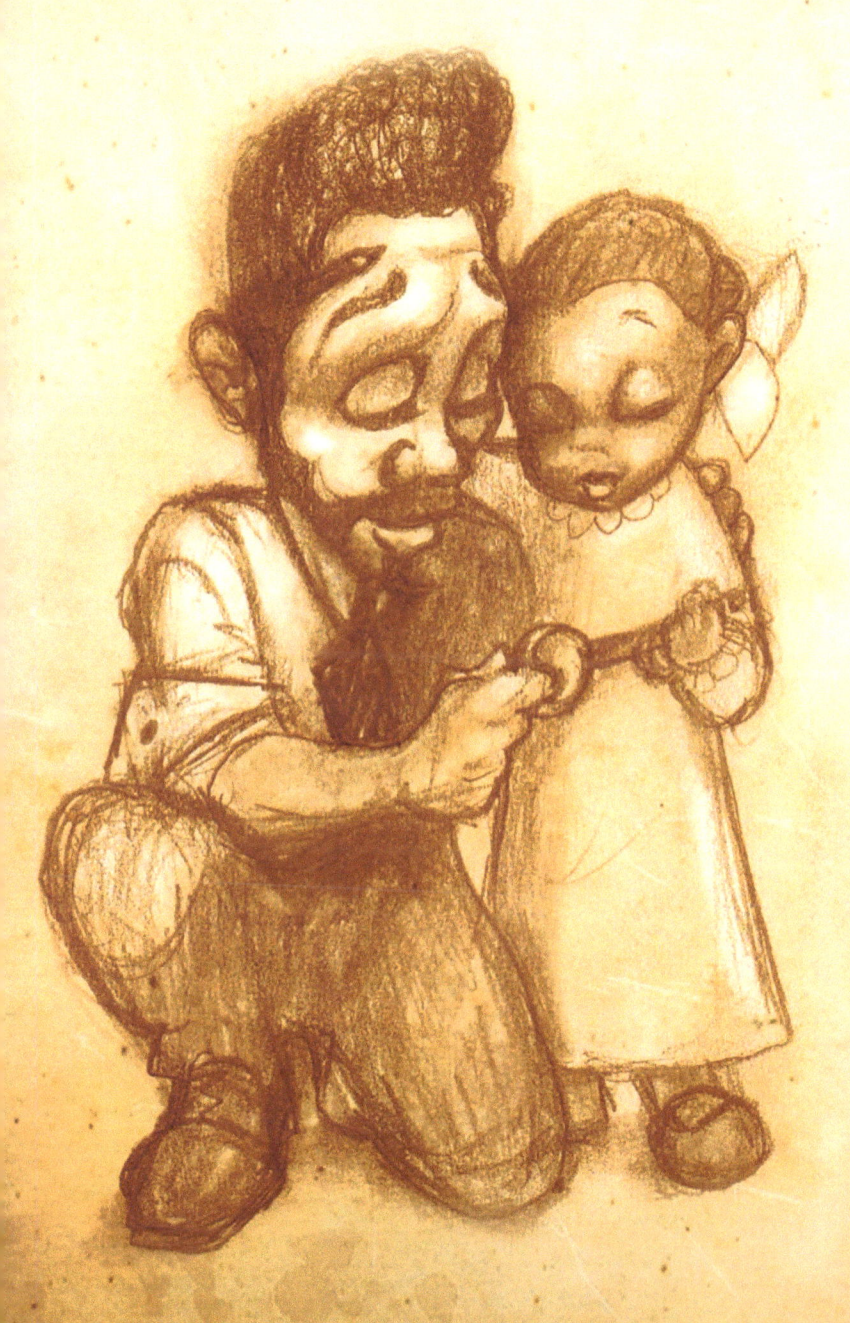

33

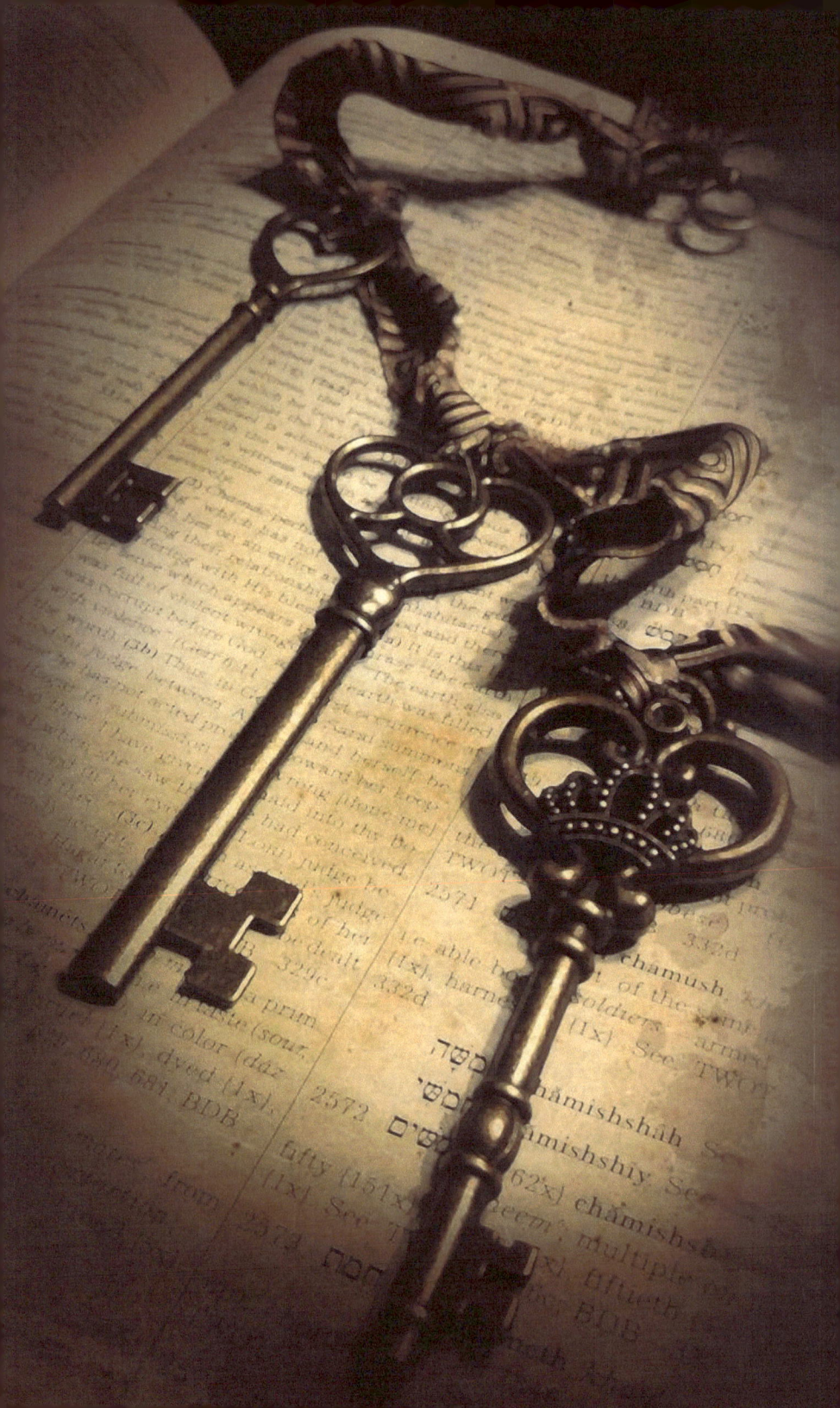

Creative Key Number 3

Your creative ability and talent is a gift FROM God given specifically TO you for the benefit of OTHERS.

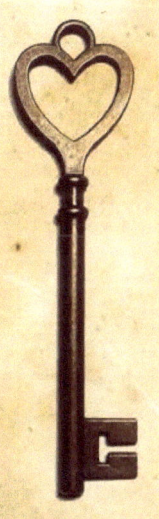

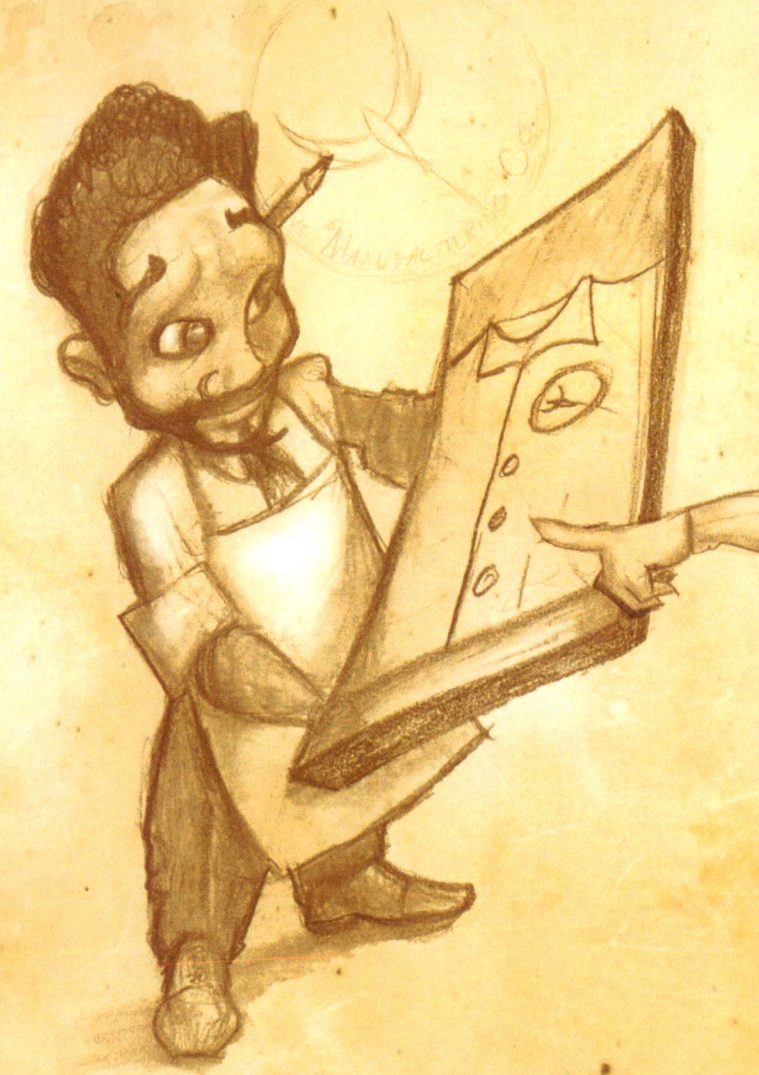

"Your creative ability and talent is a gift FROM God given specifically TO you for the benefit of OTHERS."
-Edward B. Garrett

"Each one should use whatever gift he has received to serve others, faithfully administering God's grace in its various forms."
1 Peter 4:10

36

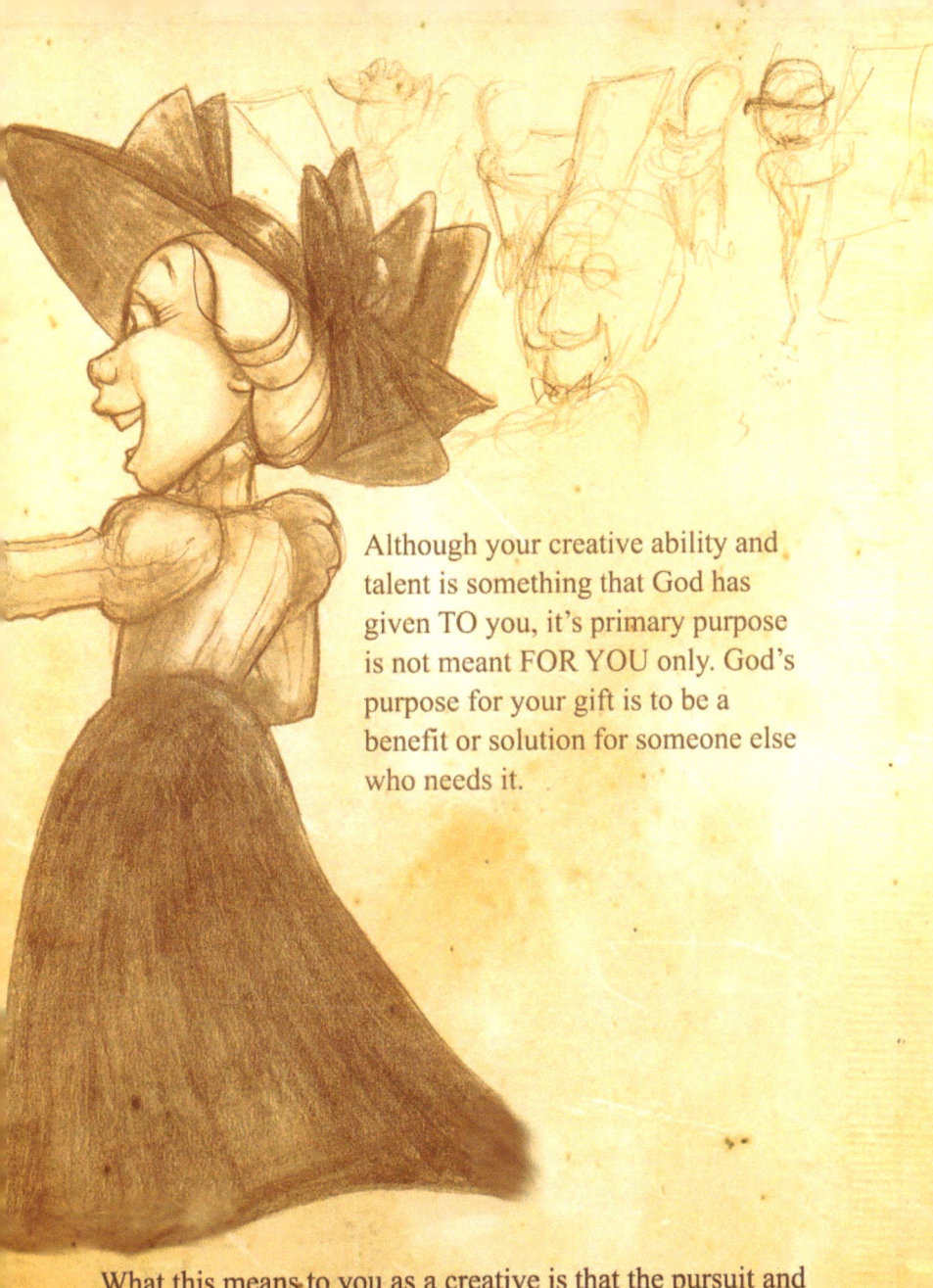

Although your creative ability and talent is something that God has given TO you, it's primary purpose is not meant FOR YOU only. God's purpose for your gift is to be a benefit or solution for someone else who needs it.

What this means to you as a creative is that the pursuit and development of your talent is important because there is someone out there who needs what you can do. God foresaw to equip you with the gift and talent that you have because He also foresaw how He needed it used to benefit others.

37

The bible shows us the following pattern:

1. God is planning on doing something that helps the needs of a particular group of people.

2. God identifies a particular person (or persons) that He wants to join Him in accomplishing the plan to fulfill the need of those people.

3. God equips the person that's joining Him in the work with the spiritual and/or physical capabilities necessary in helping the people that need it.

An example of this specific to artists would be Bezaleel and Aholiab, two artists from the nation of Israel under the leadership of Moses as told from the book of Exodus:

GOD PLANS TO HELP A PEOPLE IN NEED-
Because of God's plan for them in the Promised Land, the nation of Israel had a need of seeing the "God with us" concept illustrated. God chose to illustrate this through the Tabernacle (the tent in the wilderness where God met with His people) along with its furnishings, including the Ark of the Covenant. He chose Bezaleel and Aholiab to be the artists that would create the tabernacle and its artistic elements.

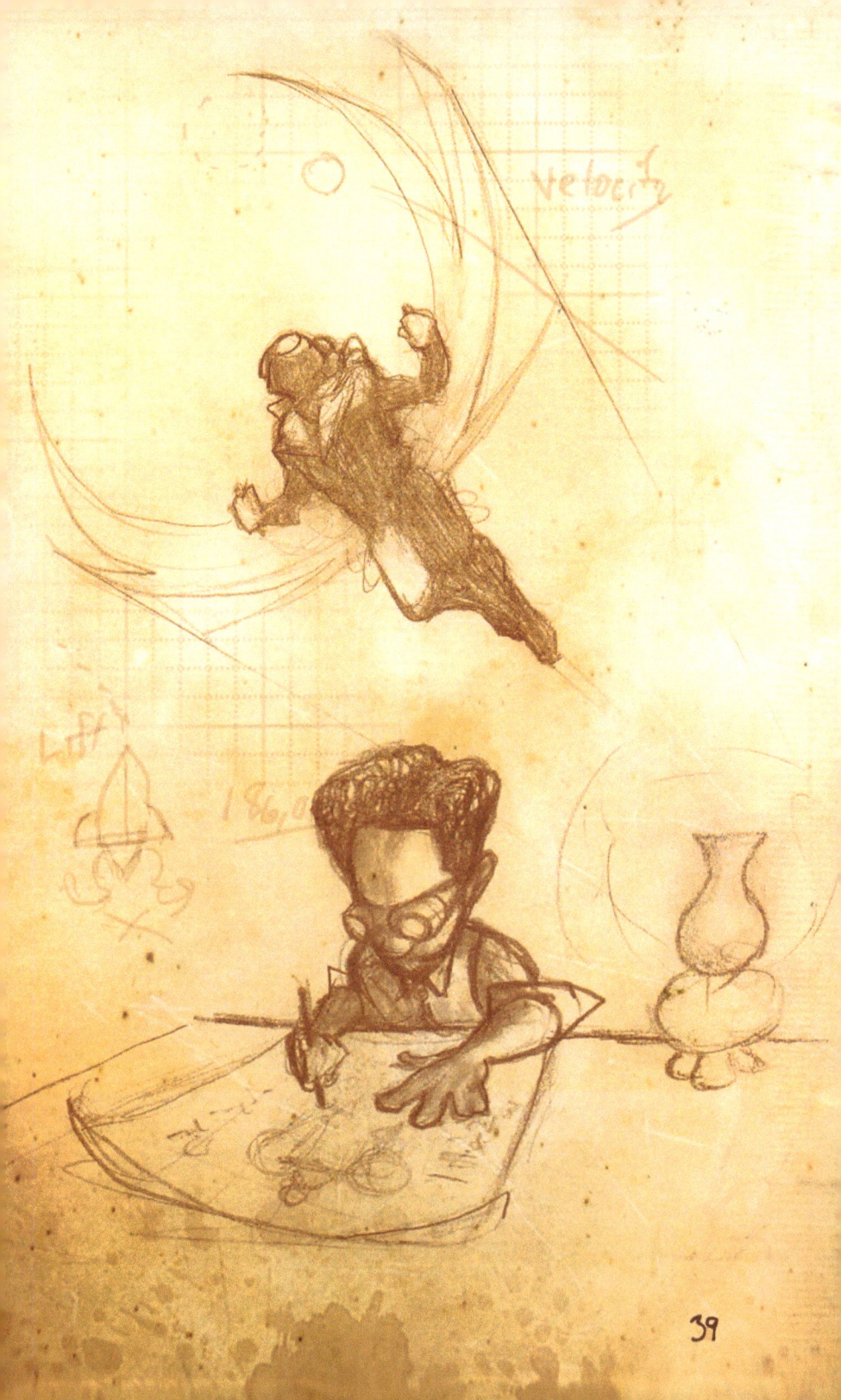

39

GOD IDENTIFIES AND EQUIPS ARTISTS TO FULFILL THE NEED-

Exodus 31:1-11 tells us how God empowered Bezaleel and Aholiab with His Spirit, in wisdom, understanding and knowledge. These two artists could have taken their gift and began using it to create whatever they wanted, but God specifically identified the primary task at hand. Their creative talent was not for a purpose isolated to themselves, but their talent was for others who needed to experience what they created.

WHAT DOES THIS MEAN TO YOU AS A CREATIVE?

Although your gift and talent can motivate and inspire you alone, its primary purpose is to benefit or serve as a solution to others. That need can be as seemingly simple as decor and design elements for their home, church or office, to more complex issues of communicating concepts through graphic design or illustration.

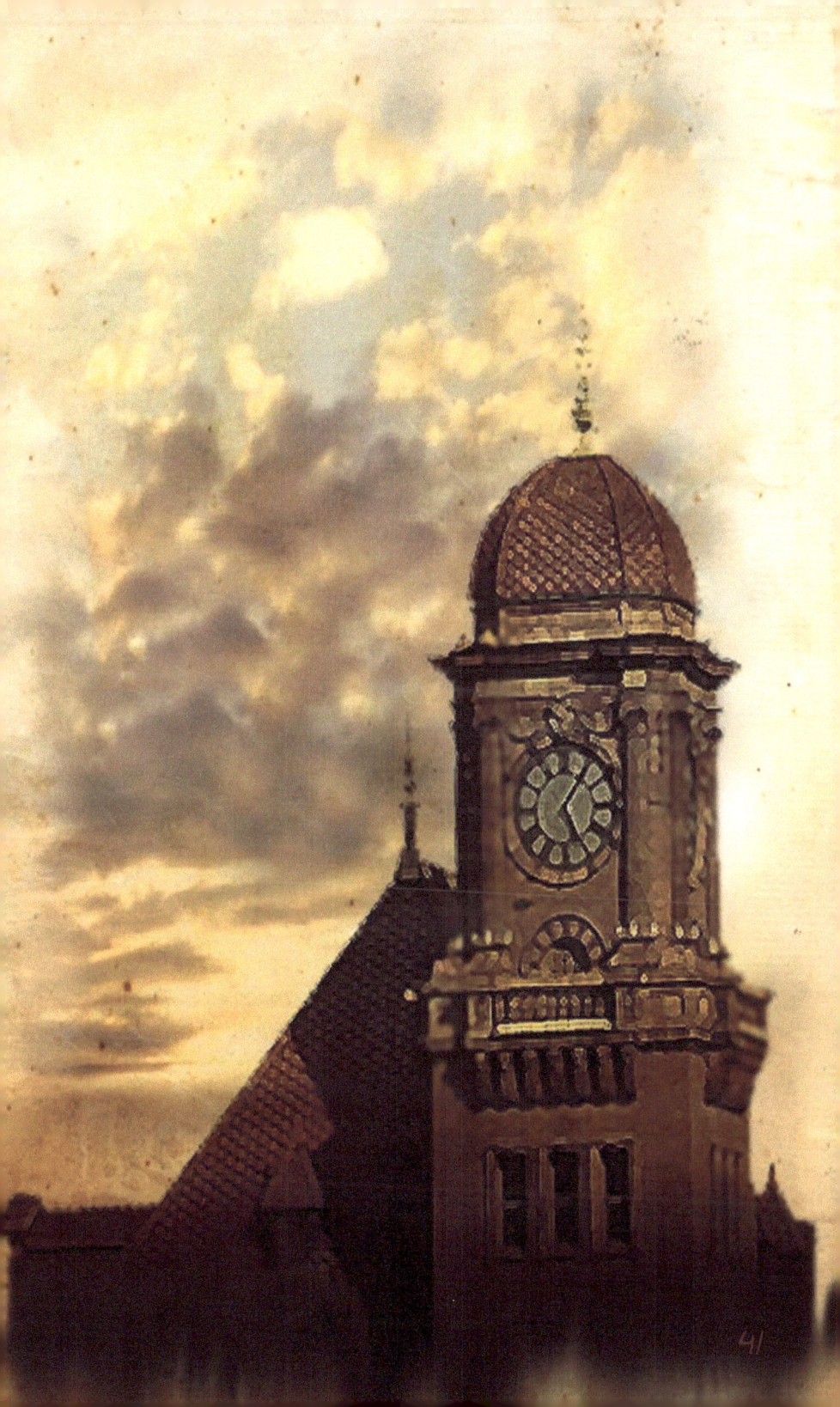

SO, WHO NEEDS WHAT YOU HAVE?

By understanding the unique capabilities of what you can
do as a creative, you will know who is in need of your
skills and abilities. If you understand that God has given
you a passion for creating comics, along with the skill and
know-how to do it, you will discover those that need to
have those comics created (readers, publishers or both). If
your artistic gift is Graphic Design, there are those out
there in need of your skills whether as an employer or
client.

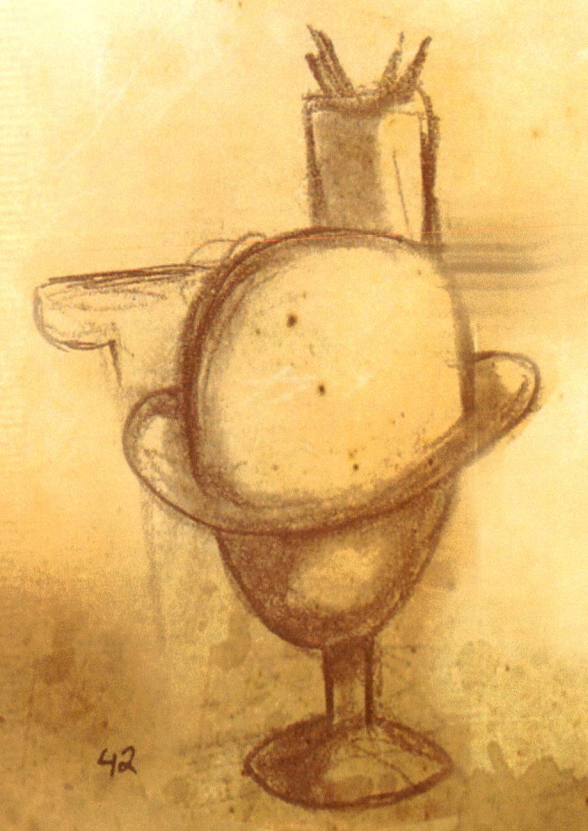

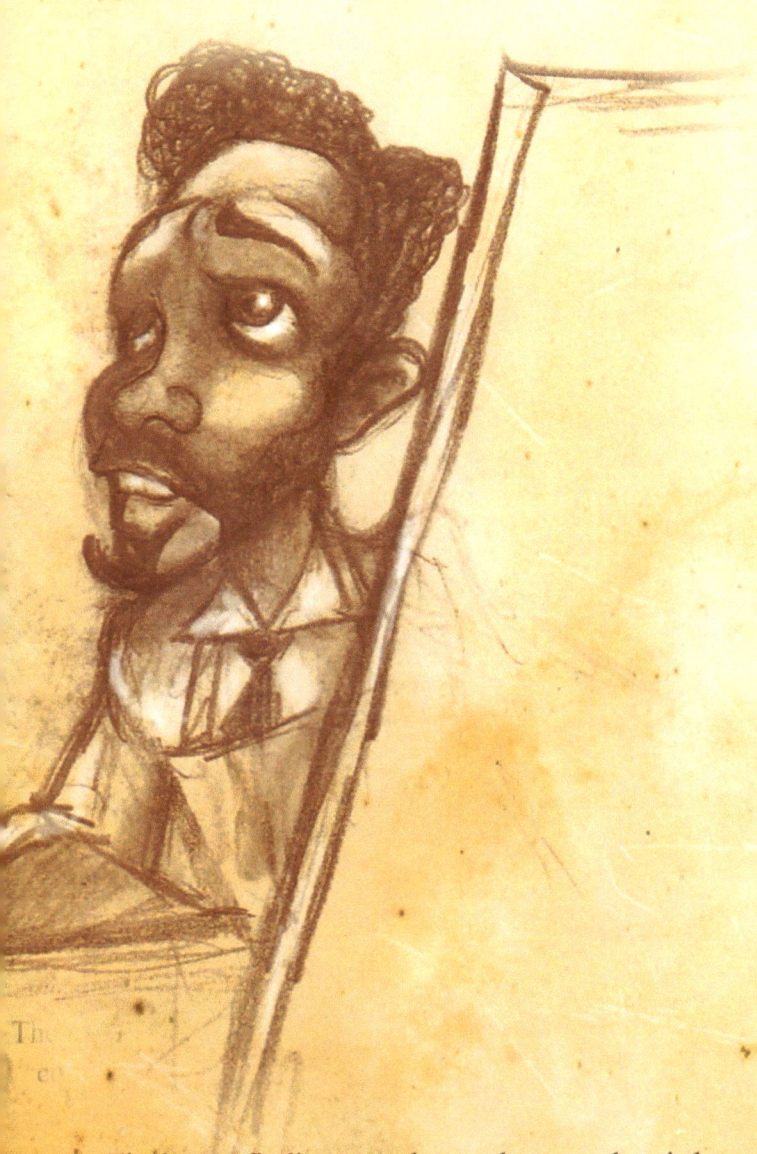

The key to finding out who needs your talent is by staying connected to Christ. Within a relationship with Christ as our Lord and Savior, we communicate with Him daily through prayer and reading of His word. Through this connection, the Spirit of God will allow you to cross paths with those that are in need of your talents.

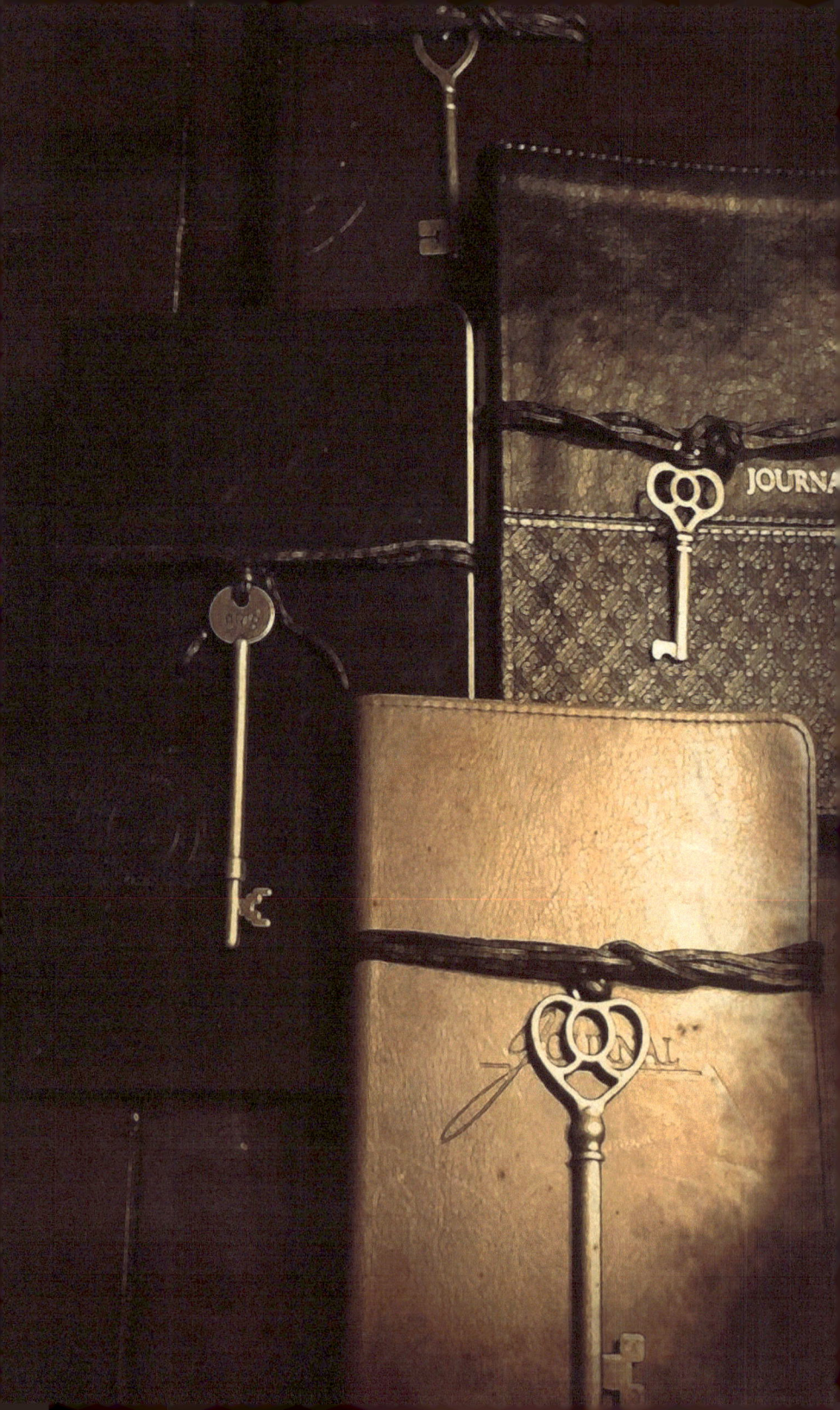

Creative Key Number 4

God has an assignment for you to complete using your creative abilities.

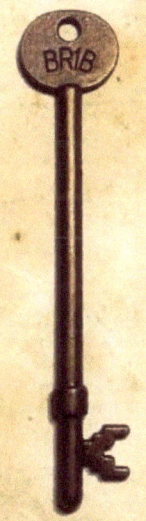

"God has an assignment for you to complete using your creative abilities."

-Edward B. Garrett

"For I know the plans I have for you," declares the LORD, "plans to prosper you and not to harm you, plans to give you hope and a future." Jeremiah 29:11

I've always said that God never does anything without reason. Everything that He does is a part of a plan. God has never created a person without having a plan and purpose in mind for that person's life. This concept really applies to the artist. God never gives a creative talent to someone without having a plan in mind for the use of that talent.

Usually, your assignment has something to do with something that you have a passion for (such as your art) or something that you really hate.

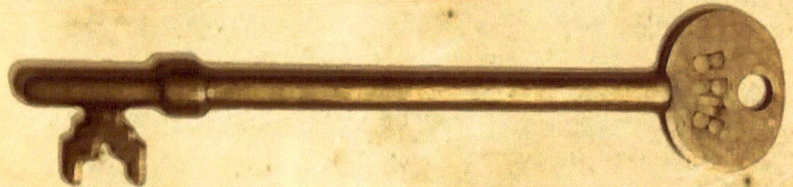

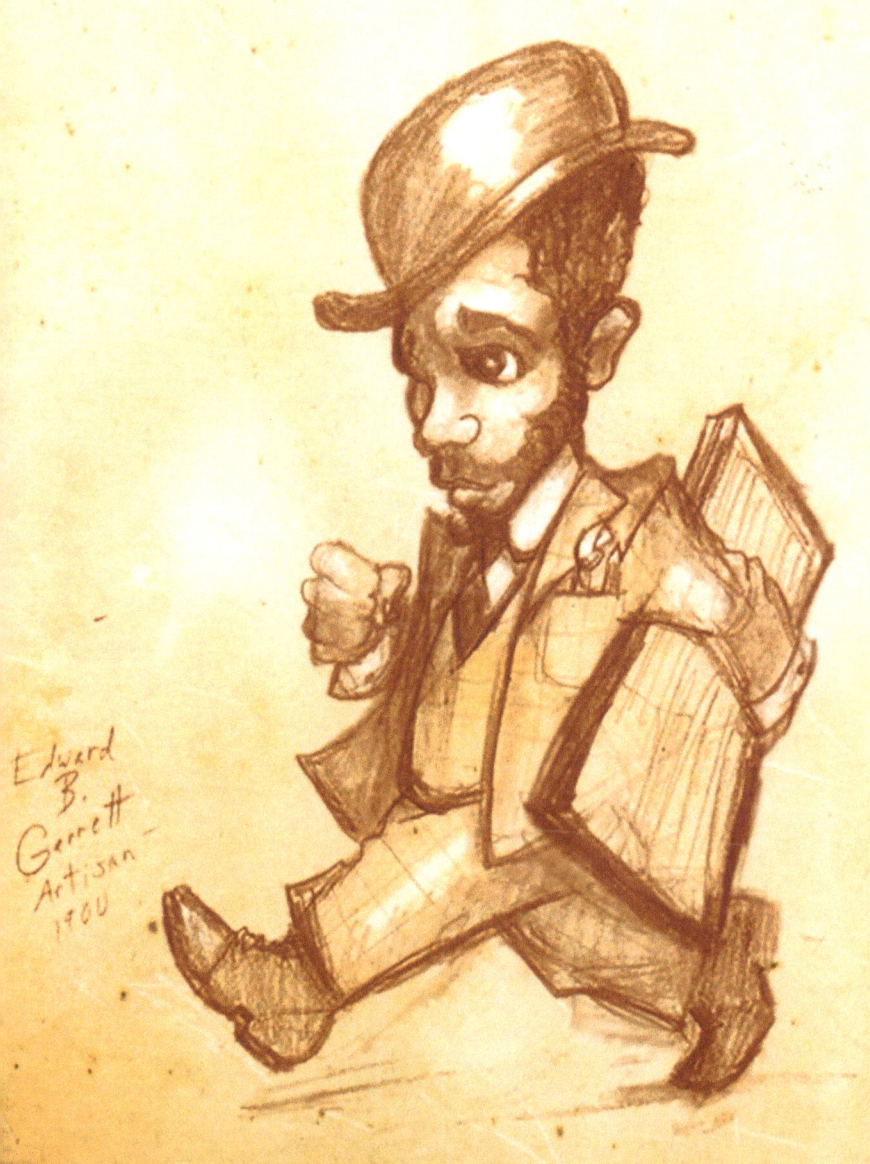

Edward
B.
Garrett
Artisan
1700

47

A burning question that all mankind has asked, "Why am I here?", relates to your PURPOSE.

How do you discover God's purpose for your life? Here are 4 indicators that can lead to you identifying your purpose. Here's my take on how they especially relate to the artist:

a. Passion- That God-given desire or burden that you can't get rid of. That thing that you would do even if no one paid you to do it. As an artist, it could be creating a series of paintings to exhibit, starting your freelance design business in order to help small businesses, or starting a Visual Arts ministry in your local church to train leaders and teach others.

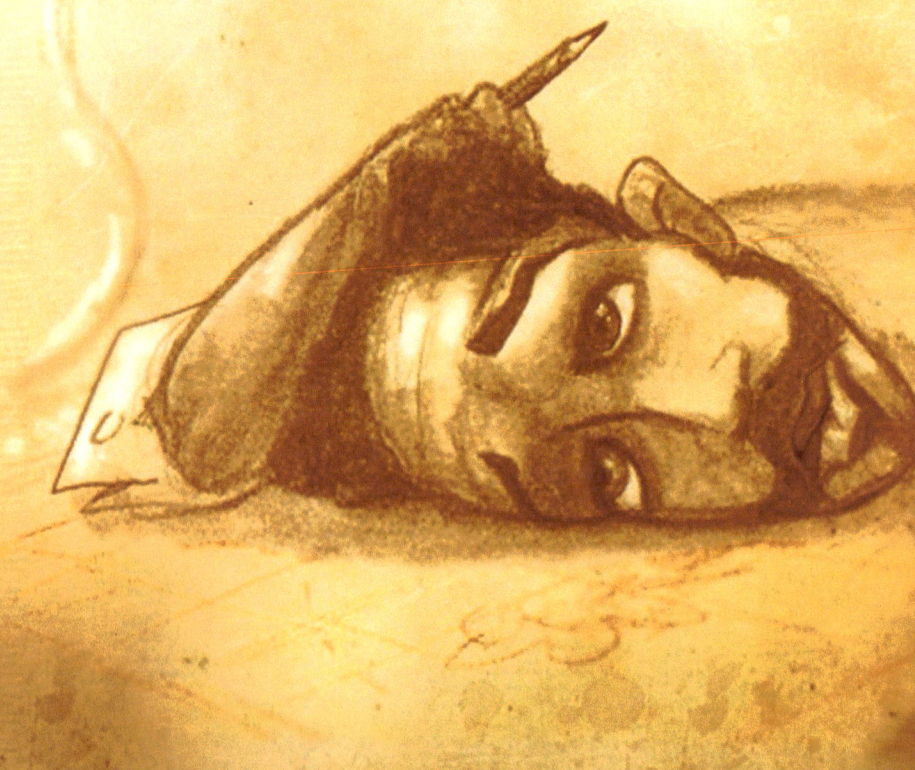

b. Ability- The skill, talent and know-how that you possess that allows you to do something exceptionally well. As an artist, this could be your basic drawing skills or your mastery of Photoshop. It could be your ability to tell a story through sequential art, or the ability to speak to a crowd as you use your art to communicate a concept.

c. Experiences- The things that have occurred or you have observed in your life, whether positive or negative, that have had an impact or have influenced your perspective.

d. Opportunities- The doors that are opening to you. Needs that you are being asked to fulfill, solutions that you have the answer to. The "Experiencing God" bible study program by Henry Blakaby and Claude King describes this as God already at work around you and inviting you to join Him in it.

Not understanding your creative purpose can lead to...

FRUSTRATION!

Always knowing that you're suposed to do SOMETHING significant, but never knowing WHAT that something is.

...is a sun and shield: the Lord will give grace and glory: no good thing will he withhold from them that walk upright...

Psalm 84:11

†

) Shadow

supply all your need
in glory by Christ Jesus
...ans 4:19

Thomas Black

Bezaleel

Creative Key Number 5

God will enable and equip you to complete your assignment.

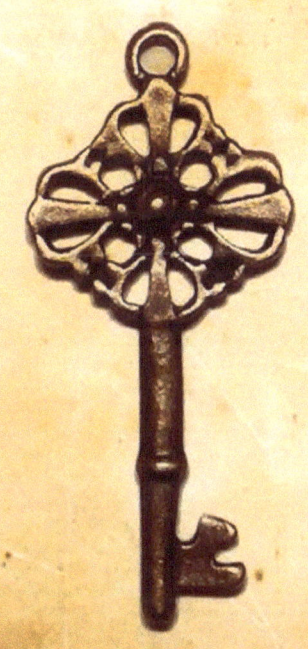

Anointed:

Being able to do
what you cannot do.

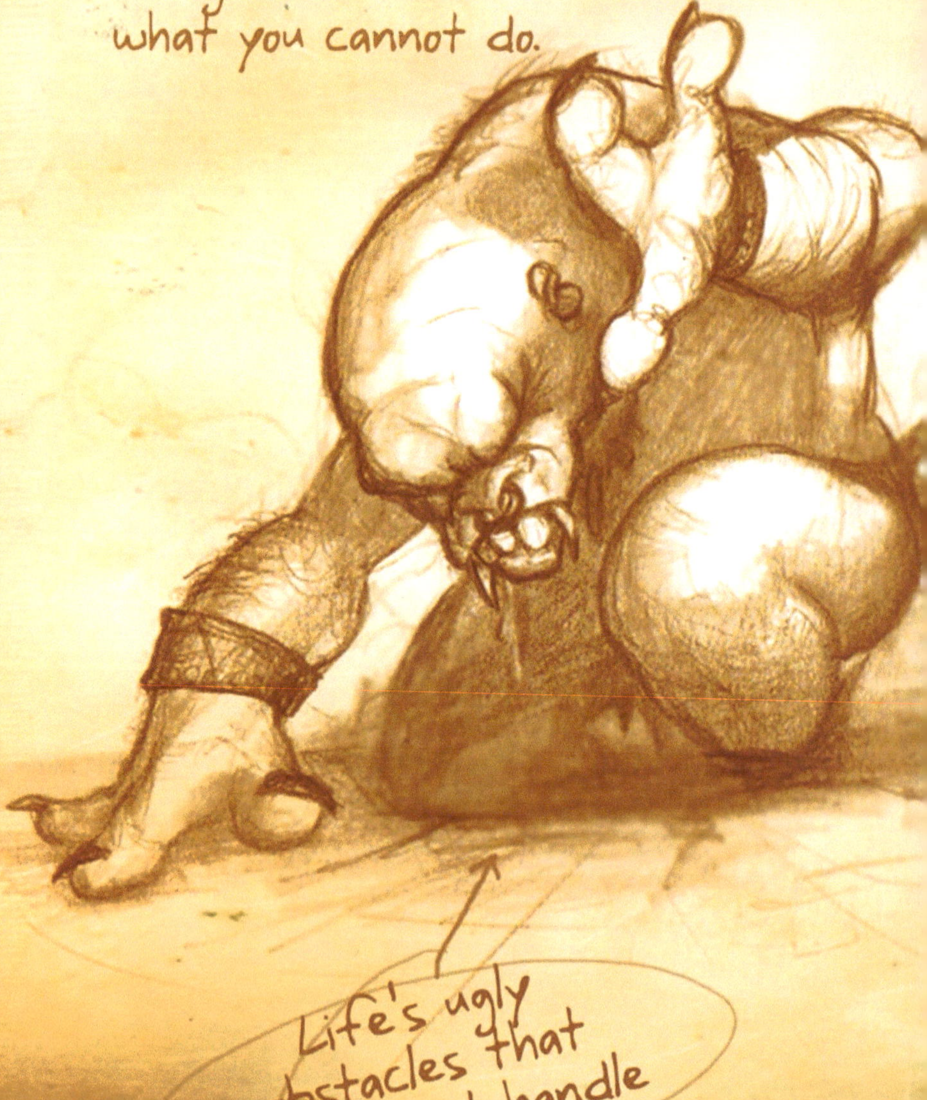

Life's ugly
obstacles that
you can not handle

"God will enable and equip you to complete your assignment." -Edward B. Garrett

A God-given assignment is often an assignment that is impossible for you to complete in your own strength.

For the Creative, this is the assignment that is:
• Beyond your skill level.
• Beyond your level of experience.
• Beyond your level of resources or finances.
• ...basically, beyond your ability to accomplish on your own!

That's where "the anointing" comes in and takes over.

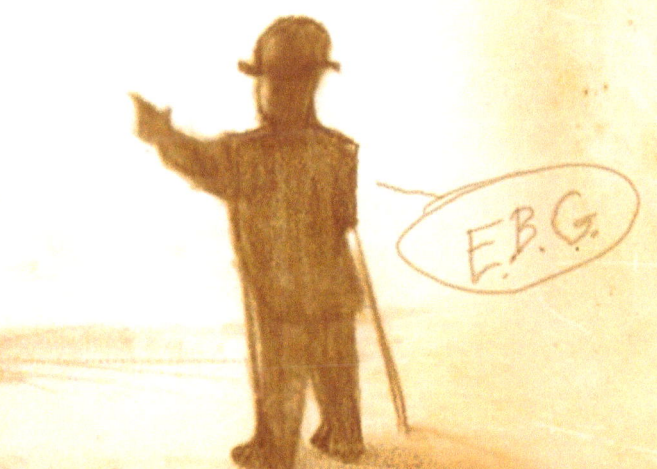

E.B.G.

Behold, I give unto you power to tread on serpents and scorpions, and over all the power of the enemy: and nothing shall by any means hurt you.

-Luke 10:19

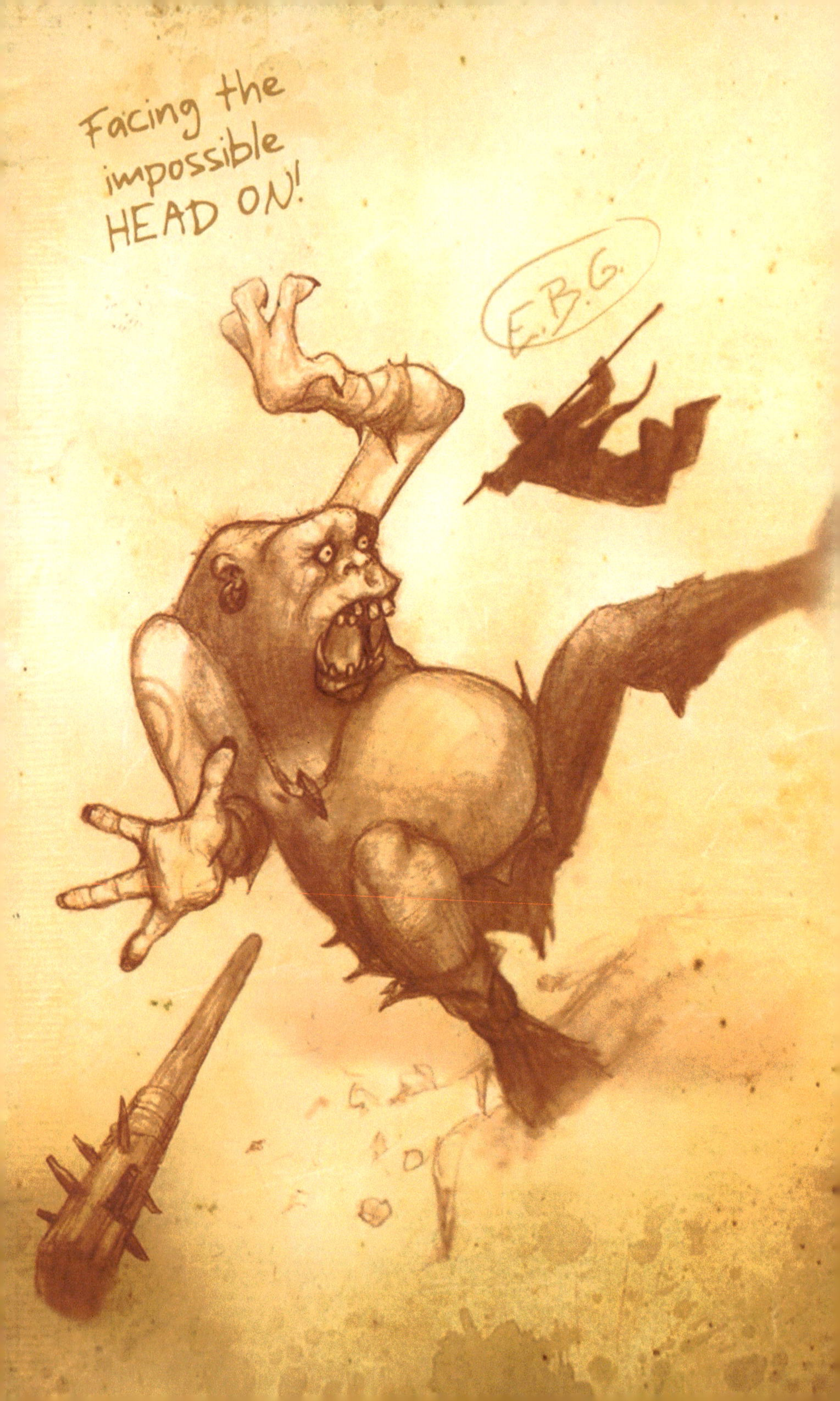
Facing the impossible HEAD ON!
E.B.G.

You may have heard the term "anointed musician" or "anointed artist", etc.
But what does it really mean?

Anointing: Raw talent, coupled with a God-given vision is one thing in the natural realm. But they take on a "super" or "above the natural" capability when touched by Christ's empowerment. "Anointing" is when something (your talent) is reserved or set aside for service to God. That service, again, is not restricted to religious-themed works, but for anything that God has planned that your talent be put to use to make a difference.

I like to say that being "Anointed is being empowered to do what you can't do."

When your creative talents touch the hearts of the untouchable, our reach the minds and emotions of the unreachable...that's where the anointing is at work.

Even when the Spirit of God enables and empowers you to take on life's issues...and you WIN...that's the anointing ("enablement") in action.

...lak (5x). See BDB—221b, 222c, 1095c

יוֹקִים {1x} Yowqiym, yo-keem', a form of
3113, Jokim, an Isr—Jokim (1x)
See BDB—220c, 222d

3138. יוֹרֶה {2x} yowreh... of
3384; sp... hence, a spri...
or autumnal show... first rain (1x), for...
rain](1x). See TW... 910a, BDB—435c

3139. יוֹרָה {1x} ...yo-raw', from
...n Isr—Jorah

See BDB—4...

3140. יוֹרִי {1x} ...rah'-ee, from...

DB 436c

3141. יוֹרָם {1x} יורם...

and one Syrian...

3142 שֵׁב חֶסֶד ...2617, kindne...
hesed, an Isr—Ju...
...b. 1000b

יוֹשַׁבְיָה {1x} Yowsh... ...aw';
from 3427 and ...ahwill
to dwell; Josibiah, an Isr...Josibiah {1x}
BDB—444a

יוֹשָׁה {1x} Yowshah, yo-shaw'; prob. a
form of 3145, Joshah, an Isr.—Jo...
See BDB—402b, 444b

...yah Yowshavyah yo-shav-yaw'...

...eating... {1x}. See TWO...

3155. זֶרַח {1x} Y...
250; ...
Zarchite) or desc—
BDB—280d, 402c

3156. זְרַחְיָה {3x} ...
fro...
...Jizrachjah,
...{1x}. Jezrahjah—
fro...

זִרְעֶאל {3...
22...

...name of t...
Jzreel {36x}

זִרְעֶאל {...
p...
...ve of Jizreel

זִרְעֵאלִית ...
...ss—Jezreelites...

3160. יְחֻבָּה {1x}
from
Isr—Jehubbah {1x

3161. יָחַד {3x} ya...
to be...
unite (2x)

Yachad mean...
"O my soul,...
their ass...
See BDB

Creative Key Number 6

If you are not connected to God, you cannot complete your assignment. Your talent becomes misused or wasted.

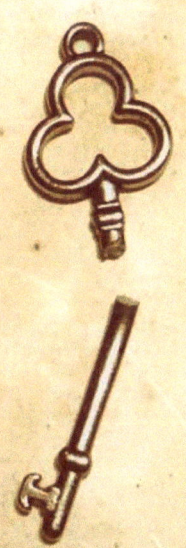

"I am the true vine, and my Father is the gardener. He cuts off every branch in me that bears no fruit, while every branch that does bear fruit he prunes so that it will be even more fruitful. You are already clean because of the word I have spoken to you. Remain in me, and I will remain in you. No branch can bear fruit by itself; it must remain in the vine. Neither can you bear fruit unless you remain in me.

I am the vine; you are the branches. If a man remains in me and I in him, he will bear much fruit; apart from me you can do nothing. If anyone does not remain in me, he is like a branch that is thrown away and withers; such branches are picked up, thrown into the fire and burned."

John 15: 1-6 ·

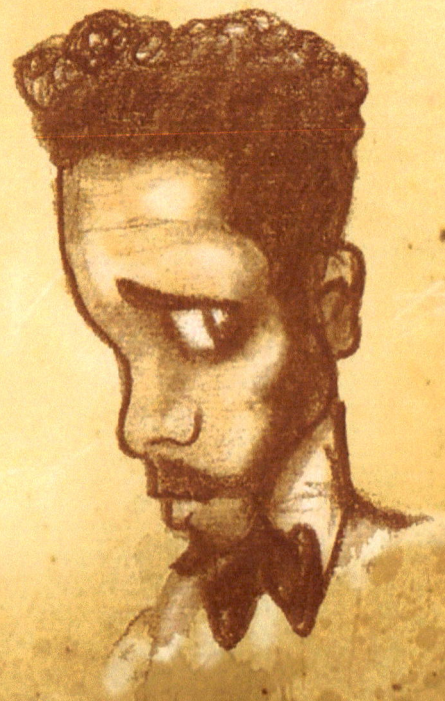

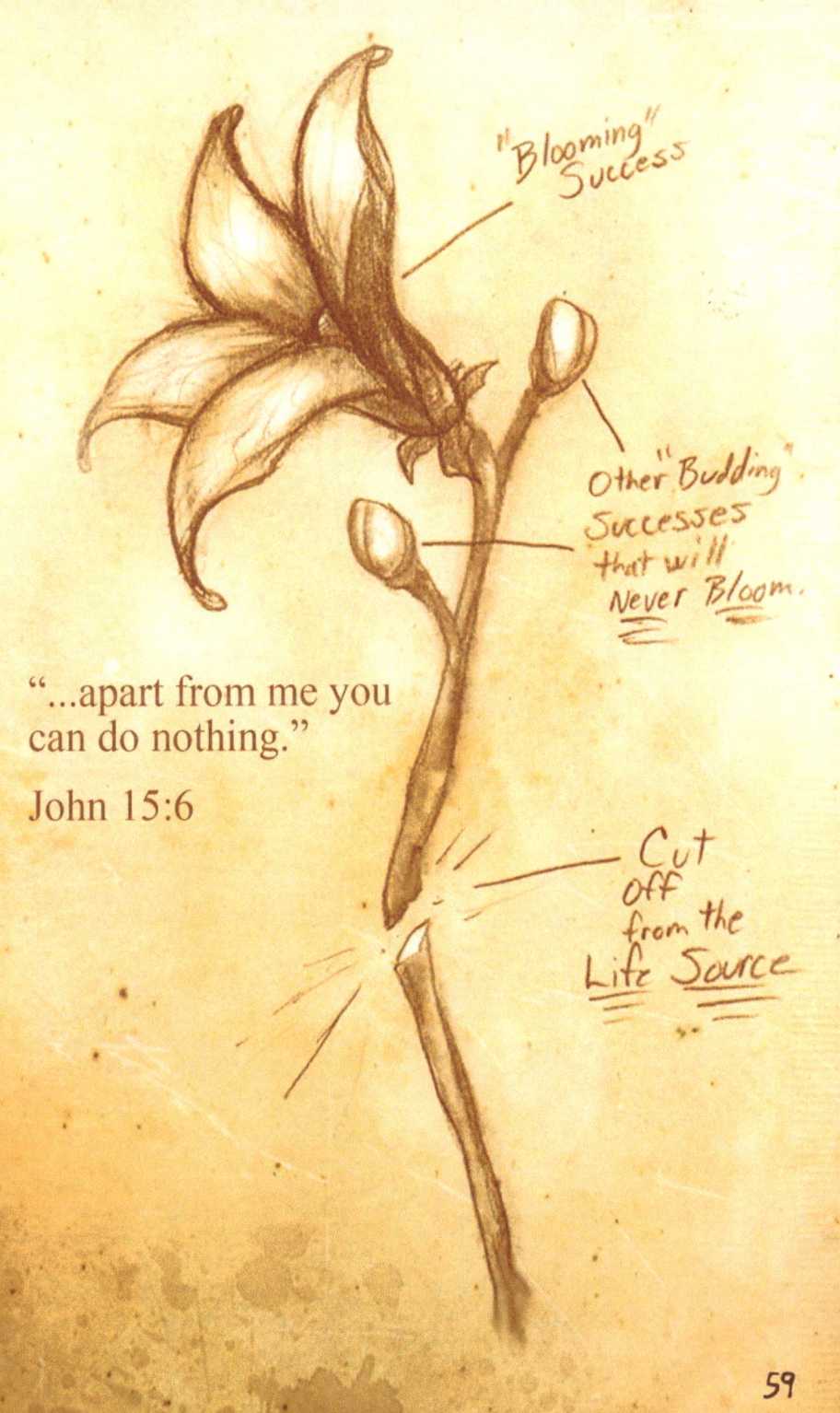

"Blooming" Success

Other "Budding" Successes that will Never Bloom.

"...apart from me you can do nothing."

John 15:6

Cut Off from the Life Source

God has given artists the raw talent to create. Training and practice help refine that talent, but when it comes to doing an assignment or accomplishing a task that God has planned involving your creativity, it can ONLY be done with the empowerment from God working with the basic talent. No matter what level of natural skill and experience an artist has, they can not accomplish something of Kingdom value (God's plan) without yielding your talent to the Holy Spirit.

There is a gap that prevents us from surrendering that natural talent to the supernatural influence of the one that created that talent. The Spirit of God is perfect in every way, yet the artist that He created and wishes to connect with is separated from Him by the inclination to reject God's way of doing things and imperfection.

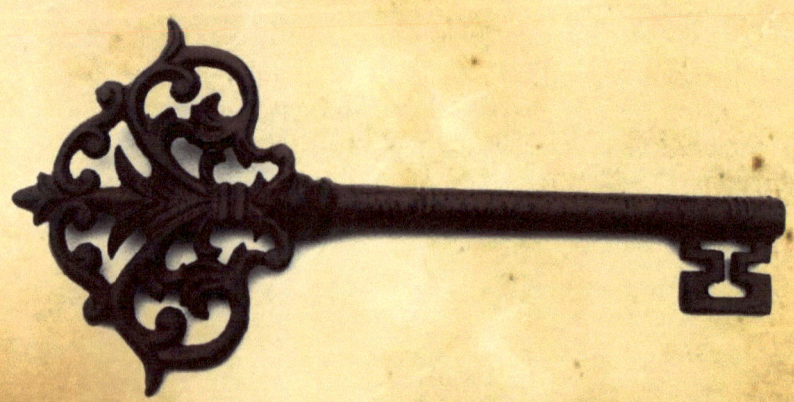

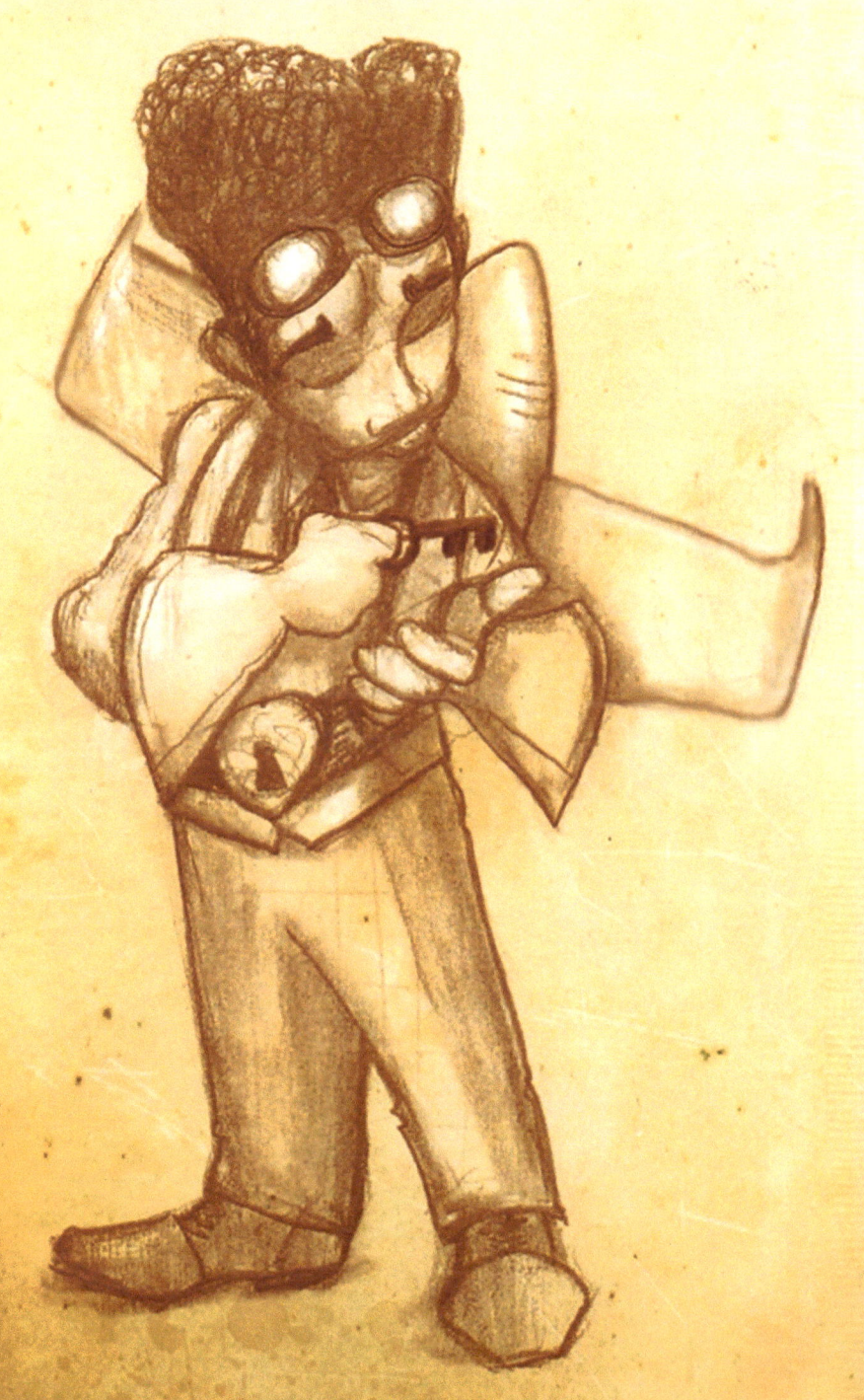

61

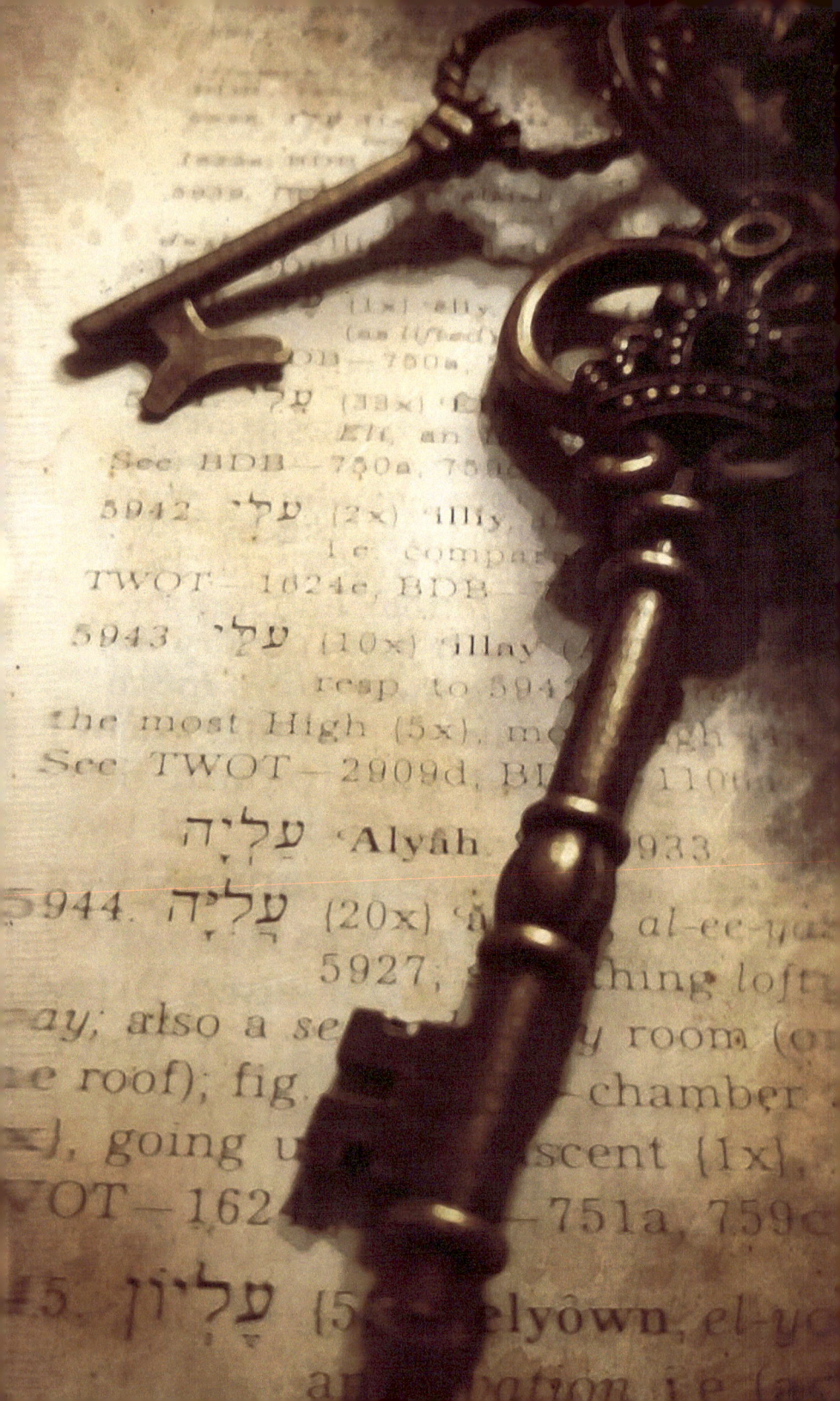

Creative Key Number 7

If you stay connected to God,
He will show you
how to complete your assignment.

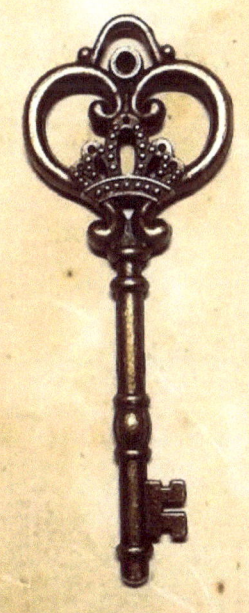

"If you stay connected to God, He will show you how to complete your assignment."
-Edward B. Garrett

"...being confident of this, that he who began a good work in you will carry it on to completion until the day of Christ Jesus.

Philippians 1:6

Although I don't want to sound like what some would call "preachy", but I must be honest. The only way to bridge the afore mentioned gap between God and the creative that He made is by accepting Christ as Savior. He was sent with the purpose of being the bridge between God, who is perfect and without corruption, and corruptible man. When the creative accepts Christ into his life, the he or she takes on a new nature.

The spirit of the creative now is connected with the Spirit of God and can be in tune with the mind of God as He directs his creativity as well as his total life.

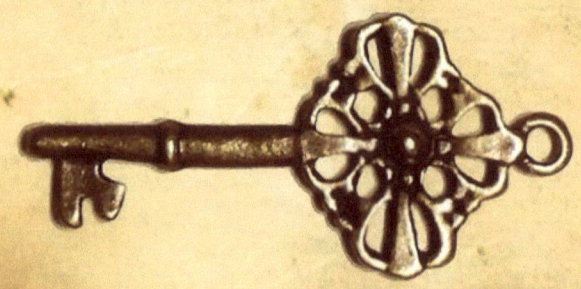

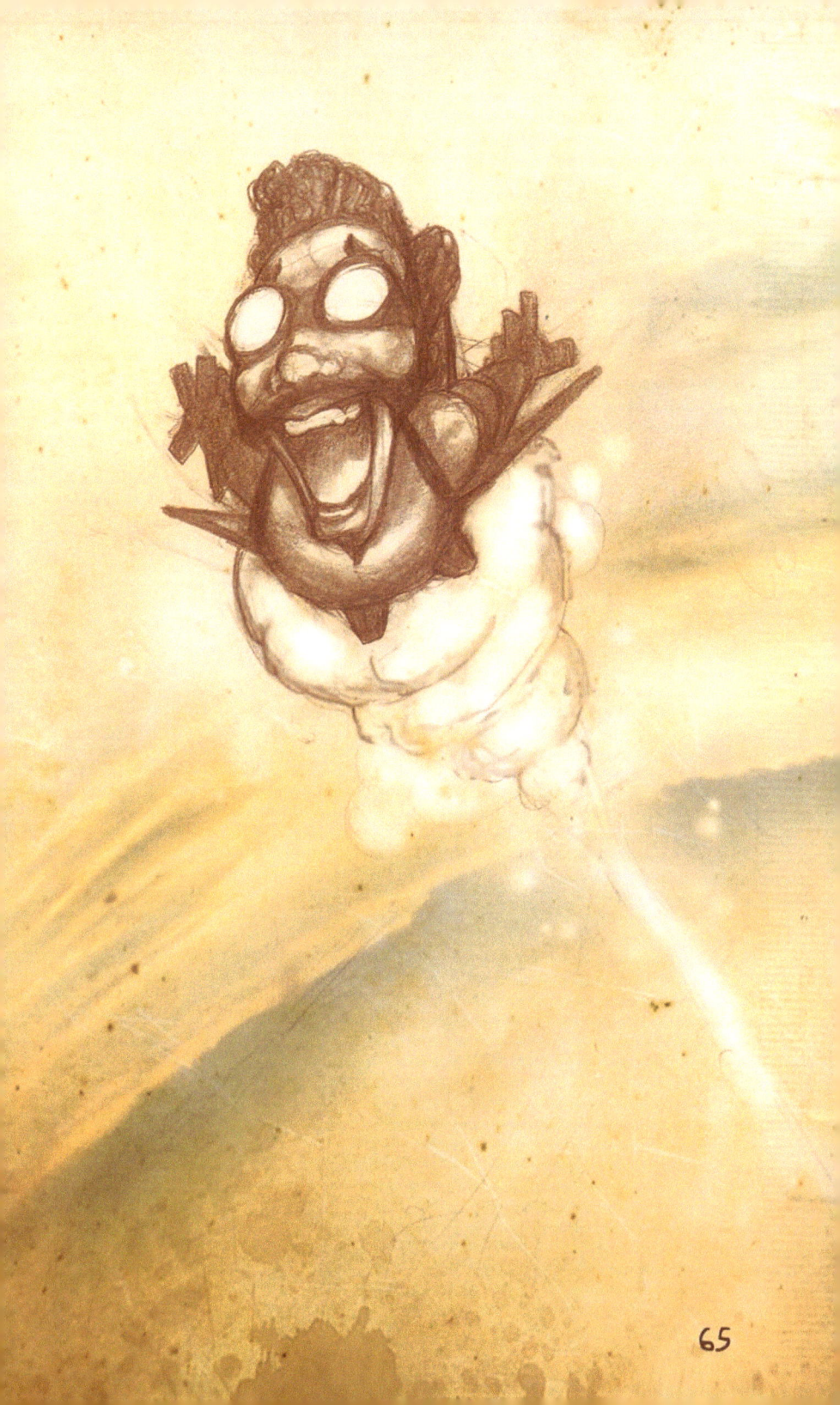

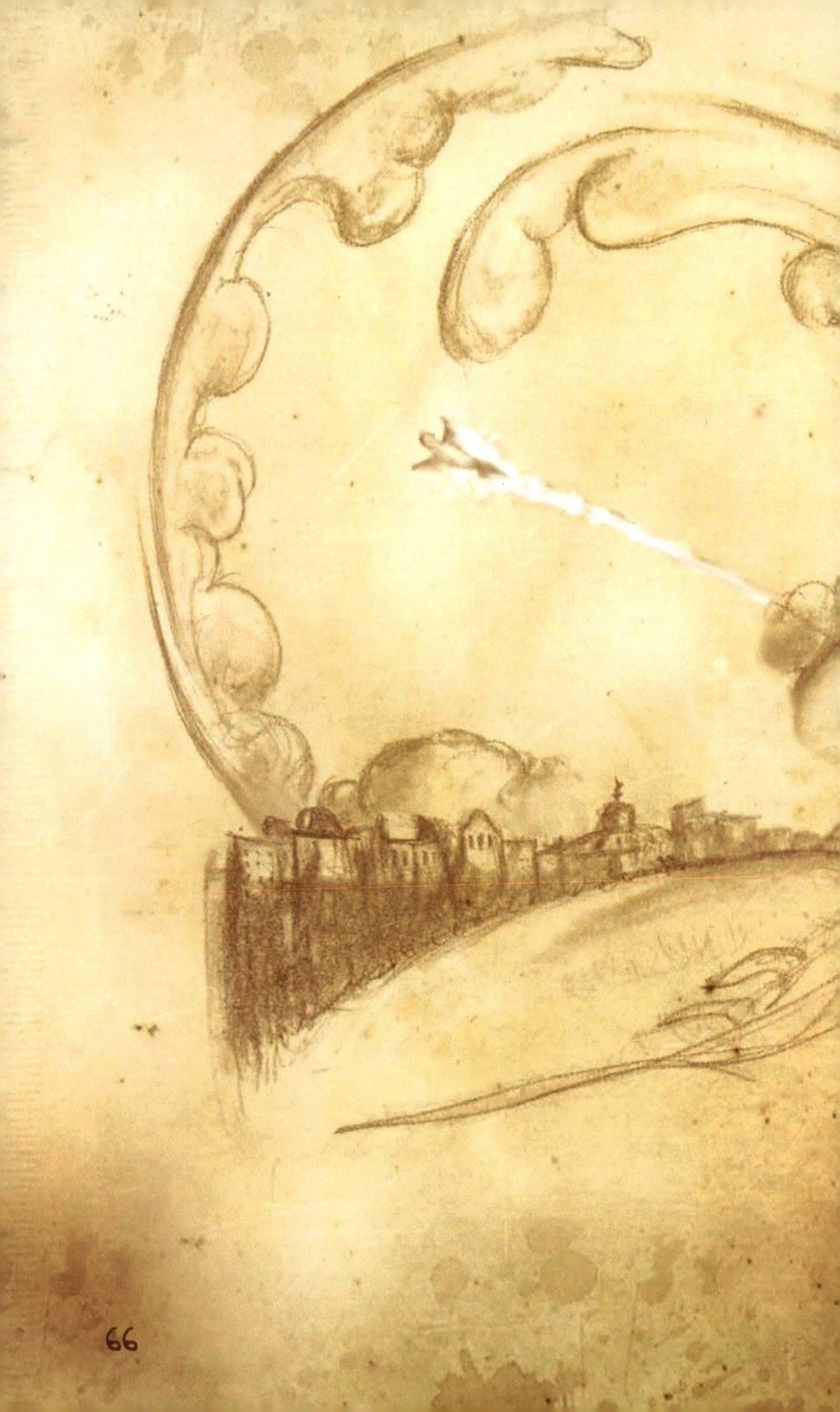

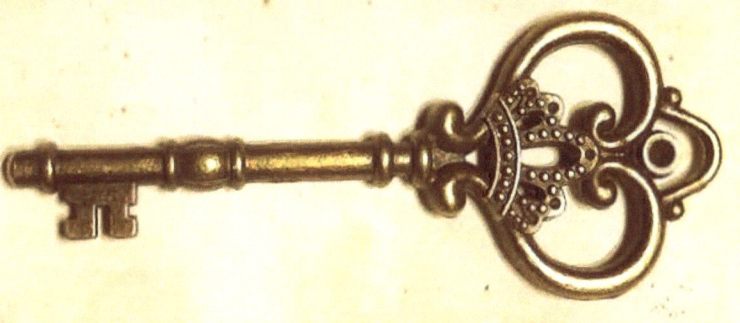

SUMMARY:

1. God is a creative God.

2. God created you in His image. He designed you to be creative just like He is.

3. Your creative ability and talent is a gift FROM God given specifically TO you for the benefit of OTHERS.

4. God has an assignment for you to complete using your creative abilities.

5. God will enable and equip you to complete your assignment.

6. If you are not connected to God, you cannot complete your assignment. Your talent becomes misused or wasted.

7. If you stay connected to God, He will show you how to complete your assignment.

About the Author

I actually had the content for this book written a few years ago, but I knew if I was to create a book for creative people, it had to look the part. So, hopefully you find the illustrations and style of this book engaging.

I've been blessed to be able to devote my time to illustrating, writing, consulting, and speaking, especially using my blog, ArtLessonsFromGod.com, as a platform.

I have been happily married to my wife Monica and I am the father of three beautiful and talented daughters: Azsa, Anisa and Moriah.

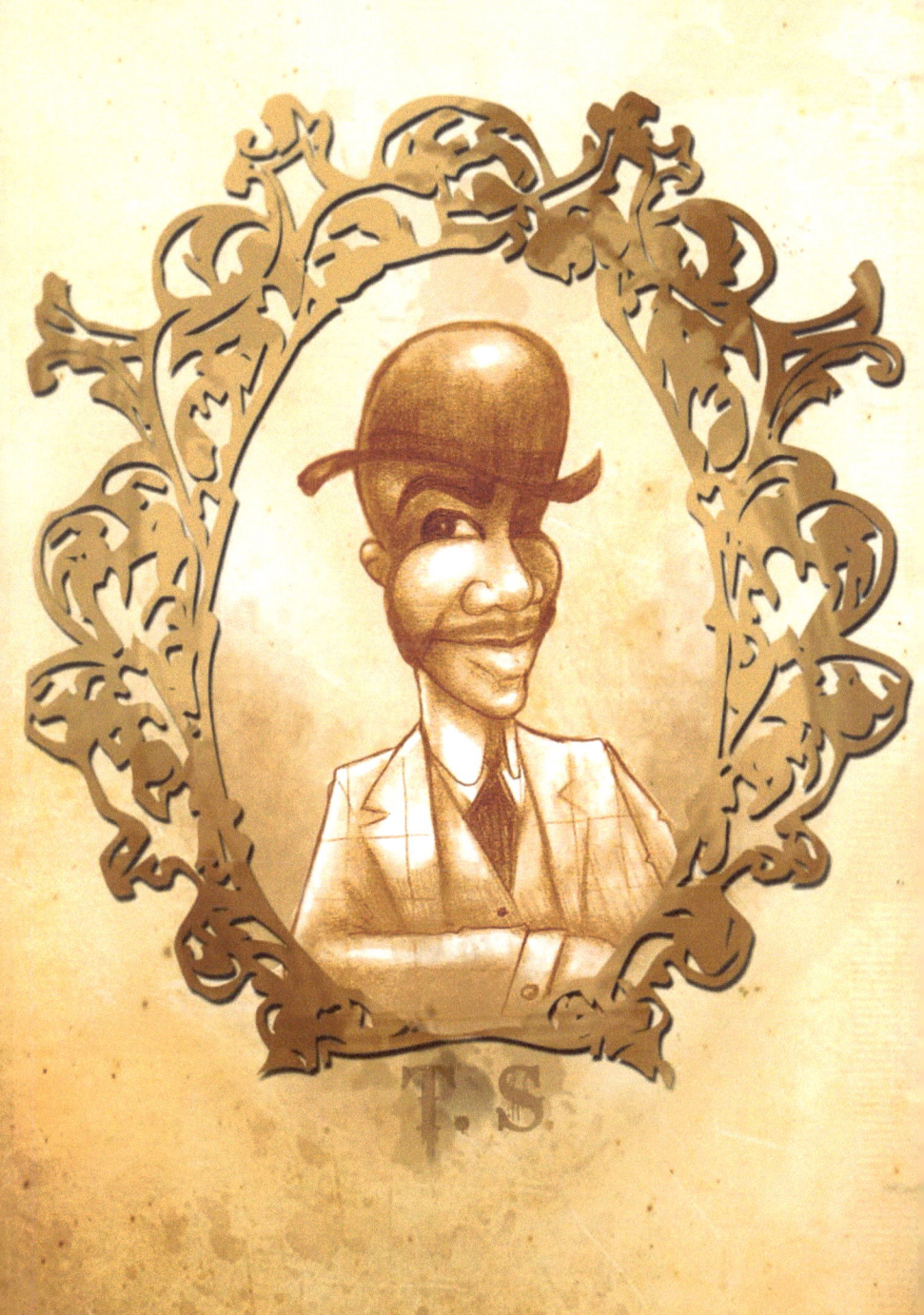